IS CHRIST DIVIDED?

A Study Of Sectarianism

IS CHRIST DIVIDED?

A Study Of Sectarianism

MONROE HAWLEY

3117 North 7th
West Monroe, Louisiana 71291

The purpose of Howard Publishing is threefold:

***Inspiring** holiness in the lives of believers,

***Instilling** hope in the hearts of struggling people everywhere,

***Instructing** believers toward a deeper faith in Jesus Christ,

Because he's coming again.

Is Christ Divided?

Published by Howard Publishing Co., Inc.
3117 North 7th Street, West Monroe, LA 71291-2227

Printed in the United States of America

ISBN# 1-878990-20-9

***"Is Christ divided?** Was Paul crucified for you? Or were you baptized in the name of Paul?"*

–1 Corinthians 1:13

Table of Contents

Introduction 1

1 What Is a Sect? 3

2 The Pharisees–Defenders of the Faith 17

3 They Walk Not With Us 33

4 Strangers in a Foreign Land 43

5 "Antisectarian-Sectarians" 55

6 Christian Unity 73

7 The Borders of the Kingdom 85

8 The Key of Knowledge 101

9 Freedom in Christ 115

10 Symptoms of Sectarianism 141

11 The Life of Grace 153

12 Anatomy of a Division..............................169

13 Focusing On Jesus 183

Introduction

What is the greatest threat to the cause of Christ today? Different answers have been proposed ranging from legalism to liberalism. Others are concerned about apathy, worldliness, humanism, division, and compromise. I suggest that the greatest threat of all is *sectarianism*.

Within the Restoration Movement, conservatives and liberals alike oppose sectarianism. Why, then, write a book about it? After all, religious journals have devoted hundreds of pages to its evil effects. One would think that it is hardly worthy of additional study. Unfortunately, a movement dedicated by its pioneers to the destruction of sectarianism has fallen prey to the malady it has opposed. It has divided, not once or twice, but often. Division is symptomatic of sectarianism. The fathers of the movement called for all men to unite on the Word of God. Their spiritual descendants have too often misused the Scriptures to fragment the body of Christ.

Regrettably, it is easier to recognize sectarianism in others than to see it in ourselves. That is why the strongest antagonists of sectarianism (in theory) are often the most rigid sectarians. We are reminded of Paul's remonstrance of the Jews, "You then who teach others, will you not teach yourself? While you preach against stealing, do you steal?" (Rom. 2:21). He might well say to us, "You who condemn the sects, will you not rid yourself of sectarianism?"

In this study we will ask some hard questions relating to the subject of sectarianism. My purpose is to identify the elements of sectarianism; and I hope that by clarifying and enlarging our understanding of the factors that contribute to the disease, we may be better able to treat it. Hopefully, those who share these concerns will build on this platform so that the prayer of Jesus for unity will be fulfilled in us.

–Monroe E. Hawley

CHAPTER ONE

What Is a Sect?

But this I admit to you, that according to the Way, which they call a sect, I worship the God of our fathers.

—Paul

Paul didn't need any more trouble! For over two years he had been incarcerated without formal charges. Distraught by the failure to resolve his case, he appealed to Caesar, and after a tumultuous voyage, now found himself in Rome. Since he didn't know who might accuse him at his arraignment, he asked to meet with the local Jewish leaders to acquaint them with his defense.

Paul's Jewish brethren listened courteously as he explained why he was in their city. When he had finished, they responded,

We have received no letters from Judea about you, and none of the brethren com-

> *ing here has reported or spoken any evil about you. But we desire to hear from you what your views are; for with regard to this sect we know that everywhere it is spoken against.* (Acts 28:21,22)

The response of the Jews was commendable in that they were willing to listen to Paul in spite of the bad things they had heard about the Christians. Men are not always so charitable with their opponents. It is noteworthy, however, that these leaders had concluded that the followers of Jesus constituted a sect. What did they mean by their use of this word? In this study we will seek answers to this and related questions as we explore the nature and implications of sectarianism.

The Meaning of "Sect"

The English word "sect" is defined as:

> 1. a body of persons adhering to a particular faith; a religious denomination. 2. a group regarded as heretical or as deviating from a generally accepted religious tradition. 3. any group, party, or faction united by a specific doctrine or under a doctrinal leader.

"Sectarianism" is defined as "the spirit or tendencies of sectarians; adherence or excessive devotion to a particular sect, esp. in religion."[1]

"Sect" and "sectarianism" have unfavorable connotations in the English language. The average person perceives a "sect" as a "way-out" extremist body, such as those led by the infamous Jim Jones or the Unification Church of Sun Yung Moon. For sociologists the term has the more specialized sense of a religious body living in tension with society.[2] Our interest in this study is to examine sectarianism from a biblical perspective.

The Greek word translated "sect" in the passage noted is *hairesis*. It is used nine times in the New Testament. The King James Version renders it "sect" five times and "heresy" four. Other versions also use such terms as "party spirit" and "faction" to translate the word. Regardless of the rendering, it is clear that the New Testament writers, at least some of the time, looked with disfavor upon the word.

Hairesis is found six times in Acts. It designates the Sadducees in Acts 5:17 where it is rendered "party" in the Revised Standard Version. "Party" is also used in Acts 15:5 and 26:5 where it applies to the Pharisees. In Acts 24:5 the attorney Tertullus applied it to Christians when he accused Paul of being "a ring-leader of the sect of the Nazarenes." To this accusation Paul responded, "But this I admit to you, that according to the Way, which they call a sect, I worship the God of our fathers" (Acts 24:14). Finally, in the verse noted at the beginning, the Jews in Rome called the church a "sect."

When these passages are taken collectively, it is clear that in Acts "sect" denotes a religious or political party. When used in this way, the meaning is neutral, that is, neither good nor bad. The speakers were simply stating the facts as they saw them. The Pharisees and the Sadducees were religious parties in the Jewish community and everyone knew it. So far as Tertullus and the Jews in Rome were concerned, the Christians were just another sect like the Pharisees and Sadducees, though an inferior one.

The other uses of *hairesis* are in the epistles. In 1 Corinthians 11:18,19 it designates divisions in the church.

> *For, in the first place, when you assemble as a church, I hear that there are divisions among you; and I partly believe it, for there must be factions [hairesis] among you in order that those who are genuine among you may be recognized.*

Though the King James renders *hairesis* as "heresies," the context shows that the church was dividing into factions or parties.

In Galatians 5:20 *hairesis* is listed among the works of the flesh. Again, the King James translates it as "heresies," though nothing in the context implies false doctrine. The Revised Standard more accurately renders it "party spirit," while the New International Version uses "factions."

This brings us to 2 Peter 2:1, the last use of *hairesis* in the New Testament. The Revised Standard reads,

> *But false prophets also arose among the people, just as there will be false teachers among you, who will secretly bring in destructive heresies, even denying the Master who bought them, bringing upon themselves swift destruction.*

The King James and the New International also read "heresies" rather than "factions" or "sects." Peter's mention of false teachers clearly implies that false teaching is involved. The issue is whether in this passage the rendering of *hairesis* as "heresies" rather than "factions" or "sects" is justified in light of the other New Testament uses. The position taken here is that while there is a definite relationship between the false teachers and their destructive teachings, what is here called "heresy" pertains to factionalism caused by the false teacher, rather than to the false teaching itself. Raymond Kelcy explains it this way:

> Peter's thought is that these false teachers will *bring heresies* covertly in a way that will deceive the unwary (see Jude 4). The word "heresy" denotes a sect or party (cf. Acts 5:17; 15:5; 24:5); it denotes schism or division (1 Corinthians 11:19; Galatians 5:20 where the R.S.V. translates "party spirit"). The adjective form of the word means "factious" or "causing divisions" (see Titus 3:10). The sectarianism brought into the

> church by these false teachers brought destruction in that it fostered licentiousness and created disregard for truth.[3]

The precise meaning of *hairesis* in this passage may seem to be relatively unimportant. After all, what difference does it make whether Paul is speaking about false doctrine or factionalism since the two are related? *The significance is this*: there are those who believe that the essence of sectarianism is false doctrine rather than the party spirit. If this is true, the remedy for sectarianism is to insure that correct doctrine is taught. If, on the other hand, sectarianism is factionalism, another solution to the problem must be sought.

False Doctrine and Sectarianism

It is apparent that much factionalism stems from false doctrine. When a church divides, there are usually doctrinal issues, even when the basic cause of the division relates to personalities. Doctrinal reasons seem to legitimatize differences that would not have resulted in separation had enough love been present.

In the post-apostolic era, and even before, false teaching found its way into the church. Leaders became alarmed and sought to combat it in any way possible. In the early second century, Ignatius of Antioch, a Christian bishop, clearly attached the meaning of "false teaching" to *hairesis*. He wrote:

> I beseech you therefore (yet not I but the love of Jesus Christ) live only on Christian fare, and refrain from strange food, which is *heresy* (emphasis mine).[4]
>
> Indeed, Onesimus himself gives great praise to your good order in God, for you all live according to truth, and no *heresy* (emphasis mine) dwells among you; nay, you do not even listen to any unless he speaks concerning Jesus Christ in truth.[5]

Both of these statements address the problem of religious error rather than factionalism. From the post-apostolic era to the present, "heresy" has taken on the specialized meaning of:

> 1. religious opinion or doctrine at variance with the orthodox or accepted doctrine. 2. the maintaining of such an opinion or doctrine. 3. Roman Catholic Church. the willful and persistent rejection of any article of faith by a baptized member of the church. 4. any belief or theory that is strongly at variance with established beliefs, mores, etc.[6]

To sum up: biblically, *hairesis* involves factionalism, the party spirit, and sectarianism. While sectarianism is often present among those who persist in teaching doctrinal error, the idea that *hairesis* is identical to false doctrine developed from the obvious relationship between factionalism and false teaching. Since factionalism is wrong and since false doctrine promotes factionalism, it is concluded that *hairesis* must be false doctrine (although the idea of false doctrine was not inherent in the word in New Testament times). This concept, developed as early as the second century, is seen in the quotations from Ignatius.[7]

Why Sectarianism Is Harmful

We now must inquire *why* sectarianism is harmful. As noted earlier, it seems that among the Jews no stigma was attached to membership in a sect. Sectarianism was accepted as normal. Though one might be a Pharisee or a Sadducee, he still recognized those of the other party as fellow Jews. He did not claim that only those in his party were true Jews.

There is a parallel in contemporary religious denominationalism. For most people, there is no stigma attached to the word "denomination." It is commonly said, "I don't believe it makes any difference which denomination one belongs to. After all, we are all going to the same place, just traveling different roads." Denominationalism is the normative state of Christianity, even though it may be lamented that all churches can't get together.

However, the teaching of the early church did not allow any such "live and let live" theology. Among the early Christians, *hairesis* assumed a negative connotation. The German theologian, Heinrich Schlier, observes:

> The basis of the Christian concept of 'hairesis' is to be found in the new situation created by the introduction of the Christian 'ecclesia' [church]. 'Ecclesia' and 'hairesis' are material opposites. The latter cannot accept the former; the former excludes the latter.[8]

The reason that this is true is that the Scriptures picture the church as a unified body which cannot tolerate division. Sectarianism is division. The church must have organic and spiritual unity.

Notice some Scriptures which stress the unity ideal:

> *For just as the body is one and has many members, and all the members of the body, though many, are one body, so it is with Christ. For by one Spirit we were all baptized into one body–Jews or Greeks, slaves or free–and all were made to drink of one Spirit.* (1 Cor. 12:12,13)

> *There is one body and one Spirit, just as you were called to the one hope that belongs to your call.* (Eph. 4:4)

> *So if there is any encouragement in Christ, any incentive of love, any participation in the Spirit, any affection and*

> *sympathy, complete my joy by being of the same mind, having the same love, being in full accord and of one mind.* (Phil. 2:1,2)

These verses clearly show that the Holy Spirit regards factions in the church as totally unacceptable. If sectarianism was not particularly offensive to the Jewish community, it is reprehensible for Christians. The body concept, stressed in the epistles, pictures all parts of the spiritual body working harmoniously for the common good. Just as the foot and the hand cooperate in the physical body for their mutual benefit, so it is inconceivable that the members of the spiritual body should not also work together for the cause of Christ. It is sectarianism that prevents this from happening. In the "Declaration and Address" of the Christian Association of Washington, Thomas Campbell expressed the ideal that ought to exist in a united body:

> That although the Church of Christ upon earth must necessarily exist in particular and distinct societies, locally separate from one another, yet there ought to be no schisms, no uncharitable divisions among them. They ought to receive each other as Christ Jesus hath also received them, to the glory of God. And for this purpose they ought all to walk by the same rule, to mind and speak the same

> thing; and to be perfectly joined together in the same mind, and in the same judgment.[9]

There can be no defense of sectarianism among God's children. It should be abhorred as antagonistic to the welfare of the united spiritual body. It is an ever-present problem with which each Christian must struggle. Though one may clearly recognize its presence in others, he must first identify the malady in himself. Having removed the log from his own eye, he will then be better able to remove splinters from the eyes of others.

Footnotes

1. *Random House College Dictionary*, revised edition, 1975.

2. A good description of the sociological theory is given by Bryan Wilson, in *Religious Sects: A Sociological Study* (New York: McGraw-Hill Book Co., 1970). See chapter 2, "The Problem of Identification," pp. 22-35.

3. Raymond Kelcy, *The Living Word Commentary: The Letters of Peter and Jude* (Austin, TX: R. B. Sweet Co., 1972), vol. 17, p. 136.

4. Ignatius, *Letter to the Trallians*, 6:1.

5. Ignatius, *Letter to the Ephesians*, 6:2.

6. *Random House College Dictionary*.

7. In the early church *hairesis* became a technical term for a body opposing the *ekklesia* understood in eschatological terms. This is especially true in Ignatius and Justin (Ign., Eph. 6:10; Tral. 6:1; Justin, Dial., 51:2). But Origen returns to the old meaning of *hairesis*, using it to refer to different schools within Christianity (*Contra Celsum*, 3, 12). G. Nordholt, *The New International Dictionary of New Testament Theology*, ed. Colin Brown (Grand Rapids, MI: Zondervan Publishing House, 1971), vol. 1, p. 535.

8. Heinrich Schlier, *Theological Dictionary of the New Testament*, ed. Gerhard Kittel (Grand Rapids, MI: Wm. B. Eerdmans Publishing Co., 1979), vol. 1, pp. 182, 183.

9. Thomas Campbell, “Declaration and Address,” in *Historical Documents Advocating Christian Union*, ed. C. A. Young (Chicago: Christian Century, 1904), p. 108.

CHAPTER TWO

The Pharisees–Defenders of the Faith

Yet you are ready to kill me, because you have no room for my word.
—Jesus

Few words in the English language malign human character more than "pharisaical." Derived from the ancient Jewish sect, the Pharisees, the word denotes one who is hypocritical and self-righteous. John Reumann observes:

> The noun "Pharisee" has such a bite to it that it was officially banned in 1902 from use as a term of opprobrium in the British House of Commons, along with "hypocrite," "jackass," and "rat."[1]

Who Were the Pharisees?

Who were these Pharisees with such a bad reputation? They are mentioned dozens of times in the New Testament, especially in the gospels, where we see them as the antagonists of Jesus. Paul describes them as "the strictest sect of our religion" (Acts 26:5–NIV). Josephus, the first-century Jewish historian, said of them:

> These are a certain sect of the Jews that appear more religious than others, and seem to interpret the laws more accurately.[2]

Josephus, who often calls the Pharisees a sect, uses the term to denote a party rather than viewing it pejoratively as a heresy. In fact, he says that at one time he himself embraced that religious sect.[3] It is interesting to note that Jesus' condemnation of the Pharisees did not proceed from the idea that they were false teachers. Jesus told his disciples,

> *The scribes and the Pharisees sit on Moses' seat; so practice and observe whatever they tell you, but not what they do; for they preach, but do not practice.* (Matt. 23:2,3)

Their problem was not that they taught error, but that they did not apply the word of God in their own lives.

The origin of the Pharisees is obscure. They were likely the descendants of the "Hasidim" or "pious ones" who emerged to defend the Jewish Scriptures during the Maccabean Revolt about 165 B.C. Josephus indicates that they wore a distinguishing garb and numbered about 6,000 during the Maccabean period.[4] However, it appears that many others were sympathetic to their cause.[5]

We do not know whether they chose the name Pharisee or if it was given to them by others. The term means "separated," but it is unclear from whom they were separating. Some think they advocated Jewish separation from the nations around them because of the encroachment of Greek culture which threatened their faith.

Others believe that the Pharisees sought separation from more secular Jews.[6] It is interesting to note that these sectarians were called "separated ones," because one of the characteristics of sectarianism is separation. Of course, there is a sense in which God's children must be separate, as Peter declares,

> *But you are a chosen race, a royal priesthood, a holy nation, God's own people. . . . Beloved, I beseech you as aliens and exiles to abstain from the passions of the flesh that wage war against your soul.* (1 Pet. 2: 9,11)

However, separation of the people of God from the world is quite different from separation within the divine family.

In spite of their reputation today, there were good things about the Pharisees. They were profoundly concerned about preserving the integrity of the Old Testament Scriptures and faithfully tried to live by the Law. Realizing that times had changed since Moses, they sought to make the Law relevant to everyday living. They opposed the influence of the "good life" that Greek culture epitomized and that threatened the fabric of the Jewish faith. They were popular with the common people and, at times at least, sought to minister to their spiritual needs.

We scrutinize the Pharisees because they typify religious sectarianism. None of us wishes to be identified with that first-century party. It will help us to appreciate how contemporary sectarian attitudes develop if we objectively consider the outlook of the Pharisees.

Though the Pharisees are primarily remembered for their hypocrisy and self-righteousness, these characteristics did not sectarianize them. No philosophy or party has a corner on self-righteousness. We are interested in the Pharisees' attitude toward the Law. It was this attitude which contributed to their self-righteousness rather than vice versa.

In order to appreciate the Pharisees' perception of the Law, we must realize that the Jews had gone through a great struggle to maintain their faith, and even their identity as a people. During the Babylonian Captivity, they fought the encroachments of idolatry and pagan culture. They were sustained by their law, and when some of them returned to their homeland, it was with the resolve that the Law be preserved at all costs. The books of Ezra, Nehemiah, and Ezekiel tell that story. During the inter-testamental period, their Selucid enemies from Syria sought to destroy both their culture and their faith. This only strengthened the resolve of their religious leaders to maintain the teaching of the Law in spite of all opposition. The Law was not only the heart of their religion; it was also the bond of their nationality.

Against this background, the Pharisees emerged in the second century before Christ as the defenders of the Law and Jewish culture. But they realized that the Law had to be applied as well as defended. The great rabbis who lived immediately before Jesus, especially Shammai and Hillel, sought to determine how the Law should be applied in diverse situations. These interpretations became the oral law, which assumed its place beside Moses' written law as equally authoritative. For instance, the Sabbath day's journey, mentioned in Acts 1:12 as a fixed distance one might travel on the Sabbath without violating it, was part of the oral law.[7] In the Sermon on the Mount (Matt. 5-7), Jesus frequently said, "You have heard that it was said . . ." followed with, "But I say to you . . ." In the first statement he was often quoting the decisions of the rabbis rather than the commandments of the Law of Moses.

The Pharisees were very legalistic in their approach to the Scriptures. They were sticklers for carrying out the Law–as they interpreted it! They were far less concerned with its ethical principles. This legalism fostered the sectarian spirit, which Jesus so strongly condemned, and exhibited itself in several ways.

Distorted Doctrine

The Pharisees were doctrinally oriented. Lack of balance generated their problem. Jesus pointed this out when he declared:

> *Woe to you, scribes and Pharisees, hypocrites! for you tithe mint and dill and cummin, and have neglected the weightier matters of the law, justice and mercy and faith; these you ought to have done, without neglecting the others. You blind guides, straining out a gnat and swallowing a camel.* (Matt. 23:23,24)

The Pharisees stressed the importance of tithing exactly as commanded. They were so precise that they even measured out a tenth of their spices. Note that Jesus did not condemn them for their tithing–even the spices. He did criticize them for majoring in minors. Tithing, though important, was less significant than the spiritual values which undergirded the Law of Moses–justice, mercy, and faith. Of what value was keeping the lesser ordinances when the vital commands were being ignored? We must realize that not all divine commands are equally important. This is clear from Paul's declaration that the facts of the gospel are of "*first importance*" (1 Cor. 15:3).

On the same occasion, Jesus showed how this doctrinal distortion caused them to look for legal loopholes in order to evade their obligations. He said:

> *Woe to you, blind guides, who say, "If any one swears by the temple, it is nothing; but if one swears by the gold of the temple, he is bound by his oath." You blind fools! For which is greater, the gold or the temple that has made the gold sacred? And you say, "If any one swears by the altar, it is nothing; but if any one swears by the gift that is on the altar, he is bound by his oath." You blind men! For which is greater, the gift or the altar that makes the gift sacred? So he who swears by the altar, swears by it and by everything on it; and he who swears by the temple, swears by it and by him who dwells in it; and he who swears by heaven, swears by the throne of God and by him who sits upon it.* (Matt. 23:16-22)

Today, citizens sometimes search out technical evasions of the law. It is not unusual to hear about someone who is obviously guilty of a major crime being released because his rights have supposedly been violated on a minor technical point. Such technicalities often pervert justice. In the spiritual realm, we ought rather to operate on the plane of righteousness. But the Pharisees kept looking for legal loopholes to help them evade the law. If a person didn't want to fulfill his promise, he could argue that he had made his oath on the temple–not its gold, or on the altar–not its sacrifice. Legally he might be correct, but spiritually he was wrong.

The sectarian spirit often dwells on details and technicalities, but may overlook the substance of the Word of God. Christians who dispute about the specifics of how the Lord's Supper should be eaten may miss the spirit that the sacred meal is intended to promote. This is not to suggest that the letter of the Word is unimportant, but something is wrong when it becomes more important than the state of the heart. Moreover, an extreme emphasis on perfect obedience to God's commands may prevent us from seeing the grace of God which is at the very heart of our faith. Many Christians feel little spiritual security because law-keeping has been substituted for grace, even as it was among the Pharisees. It is important to keep the commandments of God, but in so doing, let us not neglect the heart of the gospel message.

Traditional Interpretations

The Pharisees were traditionalists. When it came to the Scriptures, they believed that the conclusions of the great rabbis should be accepted as authoritative. Thus we read:

> *Now when the Pharisees gathered together to him, with some of the scribes, who had come from Jerusalem, they saw that some of his disciples ate with hands defiled, that is, unwashed. (For the Pharisees, and all the Jews, do not eat unless they wash their hands, observing the tradition of the elders; and when they come from the market place, they do not eat unless they purify themselves; and there are many other traditions which they observe, the washing of cups and pots and vessels of bronze.) And the Pharisees and the scribes asked him, "Why do your disciples not live according to the tradition of the elders, but eat with hands defiled?"* (Mark 7:1-5)

At the end of Jesus' Sermon on the Mount, we are informed that "the crowds were astonished at his teaching, for he taught them as one who had authority, and not as their scribes" (Matt. 7:28,29). The difference between Jesus and the scribes and rabbis was that he did not simply parrot the biblical interpretations of the great teachers of the past. The Pharisees had accumulated a body of traditional interpretations of the elders. They meticulously bathed themselves and washed all of their cooking vessels, not because of sanitation or because it was commanded in the Law, but because this was what their forebears had said the Law required. These interpretations were considered sacred. Anyone questioning them became suspect, because their oral explanations had assumed a place of authority beside the written law.

There is a tendency to elevate the interpretations of the church fathers to a place of authority beside the Scriptures. This is seen in present-day declarations that we must hold to what great preachers of the past have always taught and that those interpretations which are different from their conclusions should be rejected. One writer, in responding to such an assertion, makes the observation:

> While I am not opposed to citing the views of others in support of one's position, I am alarmed by our growing tendency to elevate "scholars in the brotherhood," and dismiss out-of-hand those views which may differ from "those things which are most surely believed among us" ("us" in this instance being our "brotherhood"). When we begin to speak and act in this fashion, I am led to wonder how we differ (other than by our confident assertion that "we are right") from those who cite denominational creeds and church authorities to substantiate their interpretaions of Scripture.[8]

Interpretations Equated With Law

When the Pharisees called Jesus to task by charging that his disciples were eating with defiled hands, he responded:

> *You hypocrites! Well did Isaiah prophesy of you, when he said: "This people honors me with their lips, but their heart is far from me; in vain do they worship me, teaching as doctrines the precepts of men."* (Matt. 15:7-9)

In accusing the Pharisees of "teaching as doctrines the precepts of men," Jesus affirmed that they were making their interpretations of the Scriptures equal to the Law. All Scripture must be interpreted to draw out the meaning. This is the function of Bible commentaries. First, the Bible must be translated because it was not written in our language. There may be alternate ways of rendering a passage. Once it is translated, the words and sentences must be explained. It is not enough to say, "It means what it says and says what it means."

The Pharisees were so dominated by traditional interpretations that they could not distinguish between what the Law of Moses said and their explanations of its meaning. It is possible for us to fall into the same trap. One can feel so strongly about his understanding of biblical teaching on worship, church organization, the return of Christ, carnal warfare, or divorce, that he is blinded to alternate explanations. That he may be correct in his interpretation of a passage or a subject should never obscure the fact that his explanations are not infallible. All of us can be wrong and sometimes are. We no more have a monopoly on truth than did the Pharisees.

Sin Externalized

The Pharisees had a distinct theology of sin. They viewed sin largely in terms of external actions. One sinned on the Sabbath if he traveled more than a Sabbath-day's journey, which the rabbis reckoned at about two-thirds of a mile. However, if the day before the Sabbath one deposited some food at that distance from his home, he might declare the spot a temporary residence, and by hedge-hopping from one possession to another, travel a greater distance without sinning.[9] The intent of the heart was unrelated to the sin.

Jesus condemned the Pharisees in saying:

> *Woe to you, scribes and Pharisees, hypocrites! for you cleanse the outside of the cup and of the plate, but inside they are full of extortion and rapacity. You blind Pharisee! first cleanse the inside of the cup and of the plate, that the outside also may be clean.* (Matt. 23:25,26)

Jesus was declaring that they viewed sin only in terms of the externals. They would go to great lengths to make sure the cup was clean on the outside, but were indifferent to its inner defilement. If we do all of the things of God's law, but our attitudes are unholy, have we really pleased God?

We see an example of this distortion of sin in another condemnation by Jesus:

> *You have a fine way of rejecting the commandment of God, in order to keep your tradition! For Moses said, "Honor your father and your mother"; and, "He who speaks evil of father or mother, let him surely die"; but you say, "If a man tells his father or his mother, What you would have gained from me is Corban" (that is, given to God)–then you no longer permit him to do anything for his father or mother, thus making void the word of God through your tradition which you hand on.* (Mark 7:9-13)

The Law of Moses taught that children have responsibilities toward their parents. Pharisees, who hesitated to violate this command but were unwilling to fulfill their filial duties, would take possessions which ordinarily would be used to meet parental needs and dedicate them to God. Under such an arrangement, they could still personally use them, but technically they could not give them to their parents since they had already been offered to God. They had found a way to have their cake and eat it, too! The only reason this subterfuge was not regarded as sinful was that they did not consider the state of the heart as being related to sin. Sin was determined by external actions.

Those in the restoration tradition sometimes unconsciously measure sin in much the same way. Violations of biblical teachings regarding such matters as the correct observance of the Lord's Supper are taken very seriously in churches that may wink at covetousness. Perhaps this is because it is easier to determine that the proper form of the Lord's Supper is being observed than that a person is greedy. Few people go to the extreme of the Pharisees in counting only external sins, but if we stress the letter of the law to the neglect of the heart, we are falling into the same trap that the Pharisees were in.

Closed Minds

On one occasion the Pharisees challenged Jesus on the ground that he was bearing witness to himself. A lengthy exchange followed in which Jesus concluded, "Yet you are ready to kill me, because you *have no room for my word*" (John 8:37–NIV).

The Pharisees thought they had all the answers. When Jesus shed new insights on the will of God, they rejected them because they had no room for his word. Their minds were made up. They simply didn't have any room left for new truth. The closed mind is a common characteristic of sectarianism. It is easy to detect in other people, but much harder to see in ourselves. Disciples of Jesus must always leave room in their minds for new insights into God's word.

The Pharisees were not all bad people. Remember that Nicodemus and Saul of Tarsus were of that party. Certainly, they were ethically superior to those in the Gentile world. Judaism attracted Greek and Roman "God-fearers" like Cornelius who saw in it something far better than paganism. The Pharisees were the most prominent representatives of the Jewish faith. Their problem was that they were locked into a system that, though designed to lighten the load of the common people, degenerated into sectarianism.

We live nearly two thousand years after the Pharisees. We can study them as an ancient curiosity known for their antagonism to Jesus, or we can observe how their misguided piety is mirrored in our own attitudes. We do not have to make the same mistakes when we can profit from theirs.

Footnotes

1. John Reumann, "Introduction," W. D. Davies, *Introduction to Pharisaism* (Philadelphia: Fortress Press, 1967), p. v.

2. Josephus, *The Wars of the Jews,* I, v, 2.

3. Josephus, *The Life of Flavius Josephus*, 2.

4. Josephus, *Antiquities of the Jews*, xvii, ii, 4.

5. Ibid., xiii, x, 6.

6. Davies, p. 6-8.

7. For rabbinic expositions of Sabbath restrictions, see Eduard Lohse, *Theological Dictionary of the New Testament*, ed. Gerhard Friedrich (Grand Rapids, MI: Wm. B. Eerdmans Publishing Co., 1979), vol. VII, pp. 12-14.

8. Paul E. Jarrett, "A Response to 'A Response,'" *Gospel Advocate*, July 17, 1986, p. 430.

9. H. Porter, "Sabbath Day's Journey," *International Standard Bible Encyclopaedia* (Grand Rapids, MI: WM. B. Eerdmans Publishing Co., 1979), vol. IV, p. 2634.

CHAPTER THREE

They Walk Not With Us

Master, we saw a man casting out demons in your name, and we forbade him, because he does not follow with us.

—John

Considering the frontal attack which Jesus launched against the Pharisees, we might suppose that his own followers would be repelled by any form of sectarianism. It is paradoxical, however, that as human beings we can observe mistakes in others which we cannot see in ourselves. This was as true of the disciples of the first century as it is of us today.

Jesus and the Twelve

Even the twelve were not immune to sectarianism. Jesus had to teach them a lesson in humility after he discovered them arguing about who was the greatest. To show the nature of true greatness, he took a child in his arms and said to them, "Whoever receives one such child in my name receives me; and whoever receives me, receives not me but him who sent me" (Mark 9:37).

Perhaps because he felt the sting of Jesus' rebuke, John changed the subject saying, "Master, we saw a man casting out demons in your name, and we forbade him, because he does not follow with us" (Luke 9:49). To this Jesus responded, "Do not forbid him; for no one who does a mighty work in my name will be able soon after to speak evil of me. For he that is not against us is for us" (Mark 9:39,40).

What motivated the twelve to forbid the man to cast out demons in Jesus' name? Perhaps it was partly their own inability, a short time earlier, to exorcise a demon from a boy (Mark 9:14-29). It is easy to be jealous when others succeed where we have failed. But it is also apparent that John and the twelve were imbued with the party spirit. That the man could successfully cast out demons in the name of Jesus suggests that he was one of his followers. That was not enough for John, who observed that "he does not follow with us." In other words, the exorcist had not demonstrated party loyalty, even though he was presumably a disciple of Jesus. *He had to walk with the twelve themselves to be an acceptable follower of Jesus.* The issue was not whether the man was right, but whether he had lined up with the right people. This was the sectarian spirit which even the patient teaching of Jesus had not yet eradicated from his inner circle.

The response of Jesus revealed that if the man was working in his name, he could not also be working against him. There is no room for neutrality among disciples of Jesus.

Carnality at Corinth

The establishment of the church after the ascension of Jesus did not remove sectarianism from his followers. We sometimes idealize the unity of the early church because it had not yet fragmented into present-day denominationalism. The fact is, though, that the first Christians faced many of the same problems which plague us, though in different forms.

The first-century church maintained an external unity that belied its inner tensions. Such was evident in the divided spirit among the Corinthians. Paul had planted this congregation and had labored for eighteen months to develop spiritual maturity among people converted from the depths of sin. (Man's carnal nature is not instantly removed when he begins to follow Jesus, as the Corinthians demonstrate.) While in Ephesus Paul learned that the church was rent by internal discord. Unable to pay an immediate visit to address their problems, he sent the church the letter which we know as First Corinthians. In it he wrote:

> *I appeal to you, brethren, by the name of our Lord Jesus Christ, that all of you agree that there be no dissensions among you, but that you be united in the same mind and the same judgment. For it has been reported to me by Chloe's people that there is quarreling among you, my brethren. What I mean is that each one of you says, "I belong to Paul," or "I belong to Apollos," or "I belong to Cephas," or "I belong to Christ."* Is Christ divided? *Was Paul crucified for you? Or were you baptized in the name of Paul? I am thankful that I baptized none of you except Crispus and Gaius; lest any one should say that you were baptized in my name.* (1 Cor. 1:10-15)

"*Is Christ divided?*" With this rhetorical question, Paul went to the heart of the sectarianism disturbing the Corinthians–for division is sectarianism.

From information provided by Luke, we know that Apollos spent time with the Corinthians (Acts 19:1). Whether Peter had also visited the church, we do not know. At any rate, the members had chosen sides among Paul, Apollos, and Peter. The church, though outwardly united, was divided in spirit. Paul also mentions those who professed to belong to Christ. Whether they had built their own sect around Jesus or were seeking to be nonsectarian, we cannot be sure. In any event, sectarianism had made inroads. The root problem was that the members had focused on their gifted leaders rather than on Jesus. Nothing in Paul's letter suggests that any of these men had sought a personal following, and in Paul's case we know that he did his best to discourage it.

In any group there will always be leaders and followers. A problem arises when church leaders are elevated to a position of prominence alongside Jesus. Think, for a moment, of those religious bodies which bear the names of their founders. Around the names and teachings of such men, great as they may have been, denominations have developed. What should be our attitude toward spiritual leaders? Paul put it clearly when he admonished the Corinthians, "Be imitators of me, as I am of Christ" (1 Cor. 11:1). It is proper to follow good leadership, providing one does not take his eyes off Jesus. When men focus on leaders instead of Jesus, sectarianism develops around human leadership.

Sectarianism in the Circumcision Controversy

As serious as was the Corinthian factionalism, it could not compare with another difficulty facing the early disciples. The Corinthian sectarianism affected a single congregation; the circumcision controversy threatened the very fabric of the universal church.

At the time of the conversion of Cornelius, God revealed to Peter that He makes no distinction between Jews and Gentiles (Acts 10,11). Soon thereafter, the gospel was taken to the Greeks (Acts 11:19-21). Later, Paul and Barnabas embarked on their first missionary journey. They converted many non-Jews, especially "God-fearers" who were attached to the synagogue, but who had not submitted to the requirement of circumcision which would formally make them Jewish proselytes.[1] The rapid conversion of so many Gentiles posed a new problem for the church. What was the relationship between the Law of Moses and the gospel? If Christians, whether Jews or Gentiles, are "the Israel of God" (Gal. 6:16), must one become a Jew by adopting the rite of circumcision before becoming a Christian? This was the view of an element of Jewish Christians. The core issue is explained by David Chadwell:

> The view of the Pharisees, in and out of the church, was that salvation by grace made it too simple for Gentiles to become people of God. Grace made salvation too easy. The idea that a believing Jew and a believing Gentile by grace could be equally righteous before God was unacceptable. Through the law the Jews had "paid their dues"; the Gentiles had not.[2]

So militant were the Jewish Christians who embraced this position that they seriously disturbed the young Galatian churches planted by

Paul, calling forth his letter to the Galatians in response. They also caused dissension in Antioch by affirming, "Unless you are circumcised according to the custom of Moses, you cannot be saved" (Acts 15:1). This is the kind of hard-line teaching that divides churches; and it was about to have that effect in Antioch. Accordingly, a deputation including Paul and Barnabas was sent to Jerusalem to see if the issue could be resolved by the apostles without further damage.

The ensuing Jerusalem conference is described in Acts 15. The leaders at Jerusalem strongly supported Paul and Barnabas in opposition to the Judaizers. A letter was sent to the churches troubled by these issues to assure them that the Gentiles were not required to be circumcised.

Several lessons can be drawn from this controversy. The Christian faith is not a "lean-to" attached to the house of Judaism. Salvation is by faith, not by obedience to the law. But there is also another lesson. *The apostles were dealing with sectarianism.* Seemingly, those who pressed the circumcision issue were led by converted Pharisees. In fact, they are called "believers who belonged to the party of the Pharisees" (Acts 15:5). The Pharisees were highly sectarian. After they accepted Christ, they were still Pharisees with a sectarian mentality. They thought as partisans, spoke as partisans, and acted as partisans. They viewed the church as a sect within the borders of Judaism where it competed with other Jewish sects. The difference was that it was the best sect of all. Though graciously acknowledging that Gentiles could become Christians, they imposed their own set of doctrinal restrictions which circumscribed the gospel message beyond what the Holy Spirit had revealed.

While sectarianism lies within the heart of man, its causes are diverse. The circumcision issue was doctrinal. Brethren, seeking doctrinal purity, felt it necessary to push a potentially divisive issue on the ground that a failure to do so would compromise the salvation message. They appear to have been highly motivated. Nothing suggests that they hoped for any aggrandizement from their efforts. But they had come to view their own personal interpretations of the gospel message as the exact equivalent of the message itself. They had a consuming passion for doctrinal truth, as they understood it, not realizing that their own interpretations might be faulty.

The problems relating to the sectarianism with which we struggle are not new. As with John, party loyalty is still sometimes its source. As with the Corinthians, sectarian division still results when we place our confidence in religious leaders and fail to see Jesus. And as with the Judaizing Christians, sects are still born (and die) around a set of doctrinal issues to which others are expected to conform.

Footnotes

1. The "God-fearers" or "Proselytes of the Gate" accepted the ethical principles of Judaism, but not the Mosaic rituals. They met with the Jews in their synagogues and appear to have provided for Paul a major access into the Gentile community. Examples are Cornelius (Acts 10:2), the Antiochans (Pisidia) (Acts 13:16), Lydia (Acts 16:14), the Thessalonians (Acts 17:4), the Bereans (Acts 17:12), and Titius Justus (Acts 18:7).

2. David Chadwell, *Beware of the Leaven of the Pharisees* (Abilene, TX: Quality Publications, 1985), p. 54.

CHAPTER FOUR

Strangers in a Foreign Land

Beloved, I beseech you as aliens and exiles to abstain from the passions of the flesh that wage war against your soul.
—Peter

Every discipline has its own language. The theologian speaks of the "kerygma," "soteriology," and "eschatology." The average Christian has not the slightest understanding that these terms mean respectively, "the preached message," "the doctrine of salvation through Jesus Christ," and "the doctrines of the last things."

Even the Scriptures use specialized words. "Gospel," "grace," "remission of sins," and "glory" are terms that convey distinct concepts to the child of God but are gibberish to the unbeliever.

In popular speech "positive" is good and "negative" is bad, but to a physician who tests you for a disease, "negative" is good (you don't have it) and "positive" is bad (you do).

A Sociological View of Religion

Sociologists also have their own speech. They give the words "church," "denomination," and "sect" different definitions than are current in popular usage. Though the sociological view of religion differs from the biblical, it will help believers in Christ to gain an outsider's perspective of Christianity.

Early in the twentieth century, sociologists began exploring the relationship between religion and social thought. The leading pioneer in this study was Ernst Troeltsch. In *The Social Teaching of the Christian Churches,* Troeltsch sought to identify the process by which dissenting religious bodies developed out of established religion.[1] Troeltsch defined the *church* as a Protestant body having a relationship with the government. In England, for example, the state church was the Church of England. In Northern Germany and Scandinavia, it was the Lutheran Church. A body that separated from the state church Troeltsch called a *sect.*

Other sociologists built on Troeltsch's foundation, but pointed out that in America the normative religion is not the state church, but the *denomination.* They identified those bodies which refuse to conform to the accepted pattern of religious thought as sects. Thus, sociologically defined, the *church* is the state church, the *denomination* is the popular religious body, and the *sect* is that body of people which, by virtue of its strong convictions, refuses to conform to the mores of society.[2]

Sociologically, the denomination and the sect are very different. The denomination is hierarchical and conservative, meeting the needs of those who have found their niche in society and who do not want to be disturbed. The sect appeals to the lower classes, the disenfranchised. The denomination is an external organization with structure and ritual. The sect is a subjective fellowship that emphasizes personal holiness and has a strong sense of internal brotherhood. The denomination has integrated with the world and allows its thinking and positions to be shaped by the culture of society. The sect, on the other hand, lives in tension with the world and its values.

This approach suggests that a denomination is more tolerant of differing views than a sect because a sect takes its doctrine more seriously. Typically, a sect has a strong sense of identity, viewing itself as pitted against all other religious faiths. It claims the complete and conscious allegiance of its members. It may even view itself as a body of the elite. It is the sole possessor of true doctrine, correct ritual, and moral standards which set it apart, "making claim, if not always to absolutely exclusive salvation, at least to the fullest blessings."[3] Bryan Wilson points out that "The answer to the question, 'What shall we do to be saved?' determines the quality of the sect."[4] Sociologists identify many types of religious sects, ranging from those that are concerned about changing the values of society to others that focus on the individual.

The Sect-to-Denomination Process

Sociological theory also affirms that sects typically undergo a sect-to-denomination change in which they lose their original character. While the pioneers of the movement are zealous restorers (or at least reformers) of what they believe is genuine Christianity, the next generation is less committed to the position of their fathers. The second generation is often more affluent, better educated, and more concerned about making peace with society. H. Richard Niebuhr attempted to trace the process of change in the United States in *The Social Sources of Denominationalism*.[5] He explored such factors as economic well being, the clash between rural and urban society, sectionalism, and ethnic influences.

However, social scientists have discovered that not all bodies sociologically classified as sects follow the sect-to-denomination evolution. Some sects are so different from basic Christian teaching that they cannot completely accommodate themselves to society. The Church of Jesus Christ of Latter Day Saints (the Mormons) is an example of a body that has only partially made peace with society. Sociologists identify it as an institutionalized sect which has established its own community and gives reassurance and security to its members.

Our concern here is not the process, the validity, nor the ramifications of the sociological theory of sectarianism, though all of these are worth considering. Rather, we are interested in how the theory relates to authentic Christianity and what it tells us about ourselves. Again, it must be stressed that the sociological definition of "sect" is not identical to either common usage or the biblical sense.

Was the Apostolic Church a Sect?

It is important to ask how sociologists view the body of first-century Christians. Sociologically speaking, the early church was a sect. Wilson states, "Christianity itself was only a Jewish sect at the beginning."[6] The apostolic church possessed most of the characteristics which sociologists identify as sectarian. Initially, it drew its membership from the disenfranchised, including many slaves. (This should not obscure the fact that prominent people also embraced the teaching of the Christ.[7]) The primitive church found itself in conflict with the values of society. It did not see itself as an ecclesiastical organization, but rather as a fellowship of believers bound together by a covenant of love. These were people of conviction who were prepared to stand up for their faith, even in the face of death. Though part of society, they were more concerned with restoring the individual to his proper relationship with God than with reforming public institutions. They had no strikes, walked no picket lines, and did not even try to change society by cry-ing out against the pervasive evil of slavery. They were interested in the redemption of the soul to prepare it for a better life in the hereafter and were uncompromising in their teachings relating to salvation from sin. Only in Christ could salvation be found.

In one important area the early church clearly fits the sociological definition of a sect. These people believed that they were *strangers in a foreign land.* Listen to Peter's declaration:

> *But you are a chosen race, a royal priesthood, a holy nation, God's own people, that you may declare the wonderful deeds of him who called you out of darkness into his marvelous light. Once you were no people but now you are God's people; once you had not received mercy but now you have received mercy. Beloved, I beseech you as* aliens and exiles *to abstain from the passions of the flesh that wage war against your soul.*
> (1 Pet. 2:9-11)

It is a fact that the New Testament pictures Christians as aliens in a foreign land. If the Christian is true to his convictions, he will always live in tension with society because he cannot compromise his beliefs to gain peer approval. This does not mean that he will be different for the sake of being different. He will conform to the culture around him so long as he does not have to betray his principles. He will be a good neighbor and certainly a good citizen of the land in which he lives. But he will never lose sight of the fact that he is first of all a child of God and must reflect this in his daily walk. This unyielding stance is what sociologists identify as sectarianism.

Thus, it is clear that sociologically the primitive church was a sect. But spiritually–and this is what counts–it was in fact the church of God, the body of the redeemed, saved by the blood of a crucified savior.

The sociological use of "sect" to describe the early church must be distinguished from the word's current application to strict religious bodies in the Christian tradition. Initially, the apostolic church was regarded by Jews and Romans as a Jewish sect, though there is no biblical evidence that the church viewed itself in that light. Later, the distinction between Judaism and Christianity became clear. In the first century, in spite of some internal problems, the church was a united body. On the other hand, modern sects within the framework of Christianity contribute to contemporary religious fragmentation rather than promote oneness.

Secularizing the Church

A significant contribution of the sociological sect-to-denomination theory is its focus on the persistent tendency of religious bodies to surrender their principles by accommodating themselves to the world. Certainly this is nothing new. Human beings have always struggled with the problem of maintaining their spiritual identity when they become enamored by the world. The book of Judges is the account of man's continual drift away from God. It tells how time after time Israel turned to idols because "everybody else was doing it." Later they begged Samuel, "Give us a king to govern us!" (1 Sam. 8:6). They wanted to be "like all the nations" around them.

The post-apostolic church lived in constant tension with society. This was guaranteed by the intermittent persecution of the Roman emperors in the second, third, and fourth centuries. Those Christians who chose the world left the church, but the believers who stood by their convictions were strengthened by the persecution. There was a sharp line between the church and the world. In time, however, the Romans saw that they could not forcibly eradicate Christianity. They decided that if they couldn't beat them, they would join them. The Christian faith was legalized and then made the state religion. The line between church and world was erased. In the process, the distinctive nature of the message was lost. No longer were Christians strangers in a foreign land; the foreign land was now theirs, but it was not Christ's. When the church merged with the world, it lost its right to be Christian.

It is likely that at the time few Christians knew what had occurred when the church conquered Rome. The believers were so much a part of what was happening that they could not objectively see that Christians must always be strangers in a foreign land. We face the same problem in contemporary society. As God-fearing disciples of Christ, we become so captivated by the affluent lifestyle of our day that we are often unaware of the extent to which culture shapes our thinking.

The process by which the church adopts the values of society is secularization. The subtle way in which the church is corrupted by the world is described by the authors of *The Worldly Church*:

> It has always been a difficult task for the church to be in the world and yet not of the world. The secularization of the church is but one more example of that on-going struggle. Whether the church succumbs to the lure of power and prestige or more innocently seeks only a temporary and tactical alliance with modernity, the secularization of the church is a particularly insidious kind of conformity to the world.[8]

The Worldly Church continues by addressing the relationship between secularization and sectarianism in the spiritual sense:

> There is a close connection between sectarianism and secularization. By sectarian, we mean the belief that the church has been fully restored by our

> forebearers, that the American Churches of Christ are fully identical to the primitive churches in every significant respect, and that there is now nothing left to do but defend the gains of the past. Surely this spirit has characterized many in our movement.
>
> The naivete of this position makes its proponents especially susceptible to secularization. The sectarian mind, after all, is unaware of the enormous extent to which culture moulds lives, shapes faith, and even helps determine the concerns of the church in every age.[9]

It is thus apparent that secularism and sectarianism are intertwined. If a dogmatic sectarian spirit leads to secularism, secularism insures sectarianism. So long as the church is enmeshed with the world, it can never be nonsectarian in the biblical sense.

Cornering the Truth

One other aspect of the sociological theory is especially relevant in our study. When a grain trader has gained a monopoly on a kind of grain, he is said to have cornered the market. This is what Joseph did for the Egyptian Pharaoh (Gen. 41:46-57). Many bodies classified as sects believe that they have cornered the truth. The basis of this claim is usually doctrinal. While Mormons and Christian Scientists rest their claim partially on extra-biblical sources, most sects accept the Bible as their authority and believe that they alone are right. Wilson describes how sects developed out of the Protestant Reformation.

> There emerged in Christendom, often in finely-stated formulae, a distinct idea that only those who held the same beliefs belonged to the true faith and the true church.[10]

Bible-believing people agree that the written word conveys the truths that bring us into a right relationship with God. The early church possessed these truths, though not yet in the completed form that we know as the New Testament. Most sects believe that since they have access to the Bible, they also possess the same truths as the early Christians. The problem is that they often equate their interpretation of the Scriptures with the Scriptures themselves. This leads them to conclude that they alone are right, and even to the assumption that they are the only ones going to heaven. They fail to realize that human interpretations are subject to error. This is evident when we realize that many restorationist sects often disagree about what ought to be recovered. Someone has to be wrong in his biblical interpretation!

The sociological theory of religious development serves as a mirror reflecting the pitfalls faced by those who seek to be Christians only. It should help us see where others have stumbled so that we can avoid their mistakes.

Footnotes

1. Ernst Troeltsch, *The Social Teaching of the Christian Churches* (New York: The Macmillan Co., 1950), 2 volumes.
2. David Edwin Harrell, Jr., *Quest For a Christian America: The Disciples of Christ and American Society to 1866* (Nashville, TN: Disciples of Christ Historical Society, 1966), p. 12.
3. Bryan Wilson, *Religious Sects: A Sociological Study* (New York: McGraw-Hill Book Co., 1970), p. 27.
4. Ibid., p. 36.
5. H. Richard Niebuhr, *The Social Sources of Denominationalism* (Hamden, CT: Shoe String Press, 1954).
6. Wilson, p. 7.
7. New Testament examples include many priests (Acts 6:7), Saul of Tarsus, and Manaen, foster brother of Herod the tetrarch (Acts 13:1). For a discussion of the likelihood of Christian members in the royal family of Domitian at the end of the first century, see F. F. Bruce, *The Spreading Flame* (Grand Rapids, MI: Wm. B. Eerdmans Publishing Co., 1979), pp. 162-164.
8. C. Leonard Allen, Richard T. Hughes, Michael R. Weed, *The Worldly Church* (Abilene, TX: A.C.U. Press, 1988), p. 19.
9. Ibid., pp. 31, 32.
10. Wilson, p. 15.

CHAPTER FIVE

"Antisectarian-Sectarians"

Such antisectarian-sectarians are doing more mischief to the cause, and advancement of truth, the unity of Christians, and the salvation of the world, than all the skeptics in the world. In fact, they make skeptics.

—Barton W. Stone

A study of attitudes toward sectarianism in the American Restoration Movement will help us appreciate our own problems in overcoming the malady. The movement was a fusion of several back-to-the-Bible efforts on the early nineteenth-century American frontier. The most significant of these were the Reformers (or Disciples) led by father and son, Thomas and Alexander Campbell, and the Christians under the guidance of Barton W. Stone. The two movements began to merge in 1832.

Stone had a great passion for Christian unity. When the seemingly impossible became a reality and these two diverse bodies found common ground on the Word of God, Stone devoted all of his energy to cementing that union. He was editor of the *Christian Messenger*, then in its sixth year. Once the merger had begun, he invited John T. Johnson of the Reformers to share editorial responsibilities in his single-minded effort to bring about the unity to which they all theoretically subscribed.

The pages of the *Christian Messenger* reveal the difficulty with which union was accomplished.[1] Stone felt the sting of criticism from all directions as he refused to be a partisan in brotherhood disputes. The Christians associated with Stone were loosely affiliated with churches espousing similar principles on the East Coast. Collectively they were called the "Christian Connection." The *Christian Palladium*, a publication of the eastern churches, was edited by Joseph Badger, a staunch foe of the Campbell reformers. He attacked Stone for selling out to the "Campbellites." Many of Stone's longtime associates in the Christian movement also exhibited a partisan spirit and expressed opposition to the direction Stone was leading them. From the Reformers came the charges that Stone and his people were heretical. They would be acceptable only when they changed their positions to agree with the Campbell party. When he moved to Jacksonville, Illinois, in 1834, Stone found two churches: a Christian church and a Reformers church. He refused to unite with either until they had joined their forces in common cause.

Stone, a peace-loving man who exhibited the highest Christian character, was exasperated by the partisanship he saw. Finally, he wrote:

> The scriptures will never keep together in union, and fellowship members not in the spirit of the scriptures, which spirit is love, peace, unity, forbearance, and cheerful obedience. This is the spirit of the great Head of the body. I blush for my fellows, who hold up the Bible as the bond of union yet make their opinions of it tests of fellowship; who plead for union of all Christians; yet refuse fellowship with such as dissent from their notions. Vain men! Their zeal is not according to knowledge, nor is their spirit that of Christ. There is a day not far ahead which will declare it. *Such antisectarian-sectarians are doing more mischief to the cause, and advancement of truth, the unity of Christians, and the salvation of the world, than all the skeptics in the world. In fact, they make skeptics* (emphasis mine).[2]

Stone was on target in pointing out that a movement committed to the destruction of sectarianism had been affected by the very malady it opposed! The problem was that those displaying the symptoms did not realize they had a problem. The reasons for their shortsightedness becomes clear when one examines the teachings of the movement.

Restoration Opposition to Sectarianism

Religious reformation is always initiated as an effort to correct a problem. In the early-nineteenth-century British Isles and America, Protestantism was torn by sectarian divisions. The Presbyterian Church of which the Campbells and Stone were a part, had divided and then subdivided. In Ireland, before he came to the United States, Thomas Campbell ministered to a congregation of the Old-Light Anti-Burgher Seceeder Presbyterians. Each Presbyterian body drew lines of fellowship against the other factions. In Campbell's view, this fragmented state was sectarianism at its worst. In the "Declaration and Address" of 1809, which launched the movement of the Reformers, Campbell wrote:

> That division among the Christians is a horrid evil, fraught with many evils. It is antichristian, as it destroys the visible unity of the body of Christ; as if he were divided against himself, excluding and excommunicating a part of himself. It is antiscriptural, as being strictly prohibited by his sovereign authority; a direct violation of his express command. It is

> antinatural, as it excites Christians to contemn, to hate, and oppose one another, who are bound by the highest and most endearing obligations to love each other as brethren, even as Christ has loved them. In a word, it is productive of confusion and of every evil work.[3]

Again Campbell declared:

> Instead of her catholic constitutional unity and purity, what does the Church present us with, at this day, but a catalogue of sects and sectarian systems–each binding its respective party, by the most sacred and solemn engagements, to continue as it is to the end of the world; at least, this is confessedly the case with many of them. What a sorry substitute these for Christian unity and love![4]

This negative view of sectarianism was shared by those who began the Christian movement with which Stone was associated. These men had been deeply involved in the ecumenical "Second Great Awakening" on the American frontier. The largest of the famous camp revivals associated with that phenomenon was held at Cane Ridge, Kentucky, where Stone ministered to the Presbyterians.[5] In 1803, as a protest against sectarianism, five Presbyterian ministers separated themselves from their synod to form the Springfield Presbytery. In less than a year, however, they decided that their fledgling body, designed to free them from sectarianism, was actually contributing to the disease. Therefore, in 1804 they dissolved their presbytery and issued its last will and testament. In "The Witnesses' Address" attached to that document they explained their opposition to sectarianism:

> Their reasons for dissolving that body were the following: With deep concern they viewed the divisions, and party spirit among professing Christians, principally owing to the adoption of human creeds and forms of government. While they were united under the name of a Presbytery, they endeavored to cultivate a spirit of love and unity with all Christians; but found it extremely difficult to suppress the idea that they themselves were a party separate from others.[6]

It is clear, therefore, that the founding fathers of the Restoration Movement initiated their efforts in order to oppose the religious sectarianism of their day. But such a movement must have a platform. Both the Christians and the Reformers felt that Christian unity was the answer to sectarianism. Hence, they issued a call for Christians of all persuasions to abandon their denominations in order to unite in Christ. Historians are in general agreement that in the beginning the movement was primarily a unity effort.

From the start all segments of the movement were biblically based. Both the "Declaration and Address" and "The Last Will and Testament of the Springfield Presbytery" make this clear. Creeds and denominational structures were rejected as antagonistic to unity.

It was Alexander Campbell who clarified the role of the Scriptures in the movement by introducing the ideal of the restoration of apostolic Christianity as the means by which Christian unity might be realized. Beginning in 1825 he wrote a series of thirty articles in his *Christian Baptist* on "A Restoration of the Ancient Order of Things." In this he proposed how genuine Christianity might be recovered by a return to the apostolic faith. Though some have denied that the Reformation (called the Effort by its leaders) was a movement to restore,[7] this seems unreasonable in light of the impact on the movement of Alexander Campbell's restorationist teaching. Nevertheless, the twin ideals of unity and restoration were destined to coexist in a state of tension. The divisions in the movement are to be partially explained in terms of these tensions.

Restoration View of Sectarianism

However, another concept logically followed the call for unity. If sectarianism was abandoned in order to bring Christ's disciples together, a corollary was that all Christians must be nonsectarian. *But what constitutes nonsectarian Christianity*? Stone would have responded that the absence of the party spirit makes one nonsectarian. Others had a different answer.

The Reformers viewed nonsectarian Christianity largely in doctrinal terms. They believed that contemporary Protestantism was essentially correct. Since the Protestant bodies were teaching the truth on the atonement, they felt no great need to emphasize this subject. Why argue about matters on which there is agreement? In two areas, however, they saw a need for correction. One related to what Alexander Campbell called the "ancient order," or specifically, a recovery of the nature of the apostolic church in such matters as organization and worship. The Lord's Supper became a focal point of this emphasis. The other was designated as a restoration of the "ancient gospel," which meant a return to the biblical process of conversion, with special attention to the nature and role of baptism.

Walter Scott, the leader of the evangelistic explosion of the Reformers on Ohio's Western Reserve, believed that they had totally restored those elements of Christianity lacking in Protestantism. In his preface to *The Gospel Restored,* he wrote:

> In 1823 a plea for a particular ecclesiastical order was put forth publicly by Brother Alexander Campbell. This for

> distinction's sake was called the ancient order. Others had, before this time, taken the scriptures along; but this Master stroke gave a fresh impulse to religious inquiry, and, by a single expression, "Ancient Order," limited that inquiry to a very important branch of our religion as a first step.
>
> Presiding, at that time, over a church which had already attained the ancient order, or at least as much of it as seems even now to be attained, the gospel, or rather a uniform authoritative plan of preaching it, became more the object of my attention, as it may seem from a few essays published in the *Christian Baptist*; cut short, however, by the then limited knowledge of the extraordinary topic which had been selected; *in 1827 the True Gospel was restored* (emphasis mine). For distinction's sake it was styled the Ancient Gospel.[8]

Scott apparently believed that since the doctrinal deficiencies of Protestantism had been corrected by the recovery of "the ancient gospel" and "the ancient order," there was nothing left to restore. Thus, when Protestants abandoned their creeds and denominational church structures (which made them sectarian) and accepted these principles, they became nonsectarian. The logical conclusion is that nonsectarian Christianity is described in terms of the acceptance of correct doctrine.

Alexander Campbell's teaching regarding the church reinforced Scott's view. Campbell subscribed to the undenominational concept that the church is composed of the saved. He taught that the church universal is the sum total of all congregations.[9] He also believed that there are Christians in the denominations and issued a call for these people to leave those bodies.

Campbell thought that the religious sects owe their existence to the stressing of peculiar doctrines that deviate from the biblical norm. He wrote:

> A sect . . . is a section or a party of a community, whether in philosophy, politics, or religion. It is founded on some peculiar or distinctive theory, tenet, or interest, which is not catholic or universal. . . . Whatever society baptizes into this faith (that Jesus is the Christ) and builds the church upon it is catholic; and what society does not, but substitutes for it in any human opinion, speculation or experience, is, necessarily, sectarian. And he that defends these addenda and preaches them as necessary either to salvation or church fellowship is a fully developed sectarian–a heretic, in its original import.[10]

False Doctrine Perceived as Sectarianism

A study of Campbell's writings shows that he perceived sectarianism in terms of heresy or doctrinal error. The one who subscribes to a false doctrine will separate from his fellow Christians to build a faction around his ideology. Doctrinal error causes partyism, and partyism is sectarianism. Correct the heresy and you remove the sectarianism. However, he warned:

> Finally, while endeavoring to abolish the old sects, let us be cautious that we do not form a new one. This may be done by either adding to, or subtracting from the apostolic constitution a single item.[11]

Campbell's warning against forming a new sect was appropriate. It is true that schisms are often caused when someone begins teaching a peculiar doctrine that is not based on the Scriptures and draws off disciples after him. This is sectarianism. Yet Campbell's writings also reveal that, like Scott, he limited his definition of sectarianism to divisions rooted in false doctrine. *He did not come to grips with the crucial question of whether one can be biblically correct and still be sectarian because he has the party spirit.* This is what Stone meant when he lamented the "antisectarian-sectarians." Here were people who from his perspective were doctrinally correct, but were sectarian by their attitudes and party spirit.

Campbell's limited view was predominant in the movement. Later writers such as Moses E. Lard continued to define sectarianism solely in terms of division caused by heresy.[12] Among some there was a preoccupation, still apparent today, with rooting out heresy in order to be nonsectarian. Arthur Crihfield founded a paper called *The Heretic Detector and Reformer* specifically devoted to that task. In his first issue he wrote:

> After having long and devoutly studied the causes of disunion among such as denominate themselves Christians; having come to the conclusion, that, of all the evils which disturb the peace of religious society, this of HERESY or devision [sic] is the greatest, being the acknowledged source of more than a moiety of the open infidelity that infests all Christendom; and being sure, from the nature of DIVINE TRUTH RECORDED in the Scriptures, that the evil, in a good degree, may be remedied, I conclude to offer to the public a Periodical Publication devoted, for the most part, to the detection of *Heresy*.[13]

An examination of the names of the periodicals in the Restoration Movement reveals that many were designed to expose the error of those believed to be teaching false doctrine, not to build disciples up in the faith. True, false doctrine must be opposed, but when brotherhood watchdogs like Crihfield control our thinking, a sectarian mentality often follows.

During the last part of the nineteenth century, a common motto in the movement was, "While we claim to be Christians only, we do not claim to be the only Christians."[14] Undergirding this assertion was the recognition of the identity of the saved and the church. When one is saved from his sins, the Lord adds him to his church. There is no distinction between the saved and the church. This is the underlying principle of undenominational Christianity. But if this is true, it follows that God, not man, determines the boundaries of the kingdom. Among the proponents of this view were such well-known leaders as F. G. Allen, F. D. Srygley, M. C. Kurfees, J. N. Armstrong, and G. C. Brewer. These men taught that the body of Christ is broader than any brotherhood whose boundaries are circumscribed by basic agreement on a few doctrinal issues. They acknowledged that some who had obeyed the gospel were enmeshed in religious error and sectarianism. They called upon them to rid themselves of every vestige of partyism in order to be nothing more or less than just Christians.

Two Concepts of Sectarianism

We have examined two different concepts of sectarianism. One position, taught by Campbell and accepted by many today, is that sectarianism is measured in terms of truth. If one accepts false doctrine, he is a sectarian; if, on the other hand, he preaches the truth he is nonsectarian. This position is succinctly stated by Roy Deaver:

> One who–with a very pleasant and very kind spirit–contends for (strives to uphold and to defend) a false doctrine is still a *sectarian*! Further, one who–with a bad spirit, a bad attitude–contends for the truth (strives to uphold and to defend the truth) is *not a sectarian*. He would be guilty of the sin of having a bad spirit, but this is not what makes a sectarian.[15]

From this it follows that the nonsectarian church is made up of those who hold to the truth, regardless of whether their attitudes are in the spirit of Christ.

The other position measures sectarianism in terms of the people of God rather than correct doctrine, though it does not ignore the latter element. When one obeys the gospel he is saved from his sins and is added by the Lord to the church. That church, the body of Christ, is undenominational and nonsectarian. It is composed of all who have been saved from sin, regardless of who taught or baptized them. One forms a sect out of this nonsectarian body when he divides it. That may be when a false doctrine becomes the rallying point of the new sect. But it may also occur when the body is divided by factious people, even if they do not teach error. A partisan spirit causing division among Christians is also sectarianism.

These two perspectives are dichotomous. They overlap in their regard of false teaching as contributory to sectarianism. They differ about whether a factious, unloving spirit can also cause sectarianism, even when truth is being taught. If this is possible, then there is such a thing as "antisectarian-sectarians."

Footnotes

1. For a comprehensive study of the merger of the Campbell and Stone bodies, see Dean Mills, *Union On the King's Highway* (Joplin, MO: College Press Publishing Co., 1987).
2. Barton W. Stone, "Remarks," *Christian Messenger,* August, 1835, p. 180.
3. Thomas Campbell, "Declaration and Address," in *Historical Documents Advocating Christian Union,* ed. C. A. Young (Chicago: Christian Century, 1904), pp. 112,113.
4. Ibid., p. 126.
5. Richard McNemar, *The Kentucky Revival* (Joplin, MO: College Press, n.d.), pp. 19-28.
6. "The Last Will and Testament of the Springfield Presbytery," *Historical Documents*, pp. 23,24.
7. Leroy Garrett, *The Stone-Campbell Movement* (Joplin, MO: College Press, 1981), pp. 6-11.
8. Walter Scott, *The Gospel Restored* (Cincinnati: O.H. Donogh, 1836. Reprinted by Old Paths Book Club, Kansas City, MO, 1949), preface, v.
9. Alexander Campbell, *The Christian System* (Cincinnati: Standard Publishing, n.d.), pp.55, 56.
10. Alexander Campbell, "Are the Baptists a Sect?" *Millennial Harbinger*, September, 1851, pp. 522,523.
11. Alexander Campbell, *The Christian System*, p. 84.

12. Moses E. Lard, "Have We Not Become a Sect?" *Lard's Quarterly*, March, 1864, pp. 22-39.

13. Arthur Crihfield, *The Heretic Detector and Reformer*, vol. 1, 3rd ed., quoted in *The Christian*, 1837, vol. 1, no. 1, p. 146.

14. F. G. Allen, "Our Strength and Our Weakness," *New Testament Christianity* (Columbus, IN: New Testament Christianity Book Fund, 1926), vol. 2, p. 245.

15. Roy Deaver, "The Sin of Sectarianism," *Spiritual Sword*, January, 1984, vol. 15, no. 2, p. 19.

CHAPTER SIX

Christian Unity

I do not pray for these only, but also for those who believe in me through their word, that they may all be one.

—Jesus

In the late 1920s a congregation of Christians in Michigan was rent by internal discord. The turmoil, more personal than doctrinal, worsened until one faction placed a padlock on the door of the church building to keep the other out. The other faction retaliated with a padlock of its own.

The intolerable situation ended up in the courts. When the controversy came before the judge, he lectured the disputants, "You people profess to be Christians, and yet you bring your troubles to an old sinner like me to resolve. You ought to be ashamed!" One of the church leaders later remarked, "When he said that, I knew I was wrong." It is surprising that, given the teaching of Jesus on love, it took so long for him to learn the lesson.

For centuries, division has been the scandal of Christianity. It has also been the scandal of movements in the restoration tradition. A seeker of truth may well inquire, "How can people who profess to take the Bible as their guide ignore the biblical teaching on Christian unity?"

The Root of Division

At the heart of most division, either congregational or on a broader scale, are sectarian attitudes. Our study of the problems of the early Christians and those of the Restoration Movement has shown that sectarianism is the antithesis of Christian unity and is destructive of oneness in Christ. After Jesus had asked God's blessing upon his apostles, he petitioned the Father for us.

> *I do not pray for these only, but also for those who are to believe in me through their word, that they may all be one; even as thou, Father, art in me, and I in thee, that they also may be in us, so that the world may believe that thou hast sent me.* (John 17:20,21)

Surely, every follower of Jesus, regardless of his viewpoint, has to acknowledge that we must strive to be one in Christ and, in so doing, seek to abolish every vestige of sectarianism. However, it is one thing to admit the importance of unity and quite another to agree about how it ought to be achieved and then do it. Basic differences in what constitutes sectarianism stem from two contradictory perceptions of unity. Let us examine them.

Unity Based on Relationship

The first concept is that unity is grounded in a common relationship in Christ. When one is born into the divine family, he becomes a child of God. His relationship with God is that of father and son. Others born into this family enjoy the same relationship. All who are children of God by the new birth are, therefore, brothers and sisters (Rom. 8:12-17). In a human family brothers and sisters are united by their common parentage. As many differences as they may have with one another, there is still a natural unity. In the same way, we who enjoy a common spiritual parentage are born into a unity with other believers. This unity is not achieved through great effort, but is a "given." When Paul urged God's children to keep the unity of the Spirit in the bond of peace, he assumed that it already existed (Eph. 4:1-3). Whether we like it or not, we are still joined to those who are also members of our spiritual family.

Our unity in Jesus is strengthened by common beliefs, activities, and attitudes. The more we work together, the stronger should be our oneness. The closer our doctrinal agreement, the better our relationship. As we learn to love each other and develop Christ-like attitudes, the unity into which we were born is solidified.

Conversely, our unity is weakened when we disagree about doctrine, refuse to associate with one another, and fail to develop the spirit of Christ in mutual attitudes. However, in spite of differences, we still have a unity, though imperfect, with our brethren.

If this understanding of the nature of Christian unity is correct, two things must follow. First, I must acknowledge that the one with whom I disagree is my brother–without reservation! He is not my stepbrother, not my brother-in-error. He is my brother in spite of all of his imperfections, and I am his brother in spite of mine. Second, if I am estranged from my brother, I must do all I can to remove the separating barriers, whether they pertain to sinful actions, personalities, or doctrinal issues. He may not reciprocate my overtures to a closer union, but I dare not be the one to widen the breach. I make these efforts because he is my brother. Christ died for him, too! (1 Cor. 8:11). To seek to close the gap that separates us is not necessarily to compromise God's truth. Rather, it is to recognize that disunity does not please our Savior.

In order for us to be one in Christ, at least two conditions must exist. There must be a mutual attitude of love. "By this all men will know that you are my disciples, if you have love for one another" (John 13:35). If I do not recognize a fellow believer as my brother, even with his errors, I am not going to feel any compulsion to love him. But if he is my brother, I *must* love him, though I may strongly disapprove of some of his actions or beliefs. To treat him as a stranger instead of a brother is a failure to love him.

Moreover, unity in Christ, based on a common relationship in Jesus, requires communication. Greater unity is impossible without trying to bridge the gaps. It is not enough to take a you-go-your-way, and I'll-go-mine attitude toward our brother. As uncomfortable as it may be, I must do what I can to communicate with him. In the human family, brothers and sisters sometimes remain estranged for years, simply because each one is afraid to take the initiative to remove the barriers. To do so threatens one's security: he may have to acknowledge that he has been wrong. In the spiritual realm, purposeful separation with no effort to resolve the problems is no more defensible than in the human family. Just as blood relatives must demonstrate their mutual love if they are to solve their problems, so brothers in Christ must discuss their differences on a loving basis rather than confrontationally.

Unity Based on Conformity

Another perception of unity is that oneness is based on conformity. That simply means that if you and I agree with one another, we will be united. If we disagree, we cannot have unity. Amos 3:3 is sometimes cited to support this view. "Can two walk together, except they be agreed" (Amos 3:3–KJV)?[1] However, since thinking people cannot agree on all details, what are the essential areas of agreement if unity is to be a reality? Restorationists of different centuries have variously answered this question. The sixteenth-century Anabaptists called for unity in church life. They believed that there must be conformity in the way people live, with the church leaders determining what was acceptable. A member who did not agree to live by the moral restrictions imposed by the church was subjected to the ban–shunned as unworthy–so that social pressure would make him conform. There was no room for disagreement. The dictums of the leaders had to be followed because unity required conformity in lifestyle.

Some seek institutional unity. This is the type of unity found in Roman Catholicism, based on the proposition that authority is vested in the church and its leadership. While disagreement is allowed in unimportant matters, the member must accept the teaching of the church in essentials. To fail to do so, if one is vocal in his dissent, is to risk excommunication. Such institutional unity is external in that it often produces an appearance of oneness without a corresponding spiritual cohesiveness.

Still others have called for theological conformity. This requires that there must be agreement about basic theological understandings relating to such matters as sanctification or election or the nature of the return of Christ. Which theological views are perceived as essentials of fellowship depends on the interpretations and emphasis of those calling for conformity. An example is that of

Doctor John Thomas. Thomas was associated with the Restoration Movement in the 1830s but, because of differences with Alexander Campbell, left with his followers to begin the Christadelphians in the 1840s. Members were required to totally agree with his theological views.

> His differences with Campbell grew and eventually he came to the point of insisting that the central message of the scriptures was the hope of the kingdom that would come with the second advent of Christ. That event, he believed, was very soon to take place. Abjuring previous errors, he had himself re-baptised and refused fellowship to any who dissented from his teachings. Men were to repent of their sins, live soberly, and look for the glorious reappearance of Christ, whereafter the earth would be made new.[2]

Yet others, including many in the heritage of the Restoration Movement, have insisted that a prerequisite of unity is conformity in doctrinal externals. This may involve agreement on the structure of the church or what is involved in correct worship. These things can be measured, whereas such intangible matters as one's love for his brother cannot, which perhaps accounts for less attention being given to the intangibles. This view says that before Christians can truly work together, they must practice the same things. Failure to agree in these areas is a major obstacle to achieving unity.

True Unity

Of the two approaches to unity–unity based on our relationship in Christ and unity grounded on conformity–it is my conviction that the first one is correct. This should not in the least diminish efforts to find agreement in doctrinal teaching. It should even motivate us to seek sound doctrine because of the Christ we serve. If we are, in fact, united by a common spiritual birth, we will seek accord in every possible area. Realistically, though, thinking Christians have never found perfect doctrinal agreement, nor will they. The fault is not in the perfect divine Word, but in the imperfect human interpretation and application. One has but to examine the history of divisions that have torn apart disciples of Christ from the earliest times to know that most of them have resulted from efforts to achieve doctrinal conformity. This has been especially true among those using a restorationist approach to the Bible.[3] If it is important to reproduce the essence of the Christian faith in today's society, it has been reasoned, is it not also vital to agree upon these matters?

Without disparaging the importance of correct teaching, we must note that trying to achieve unity through doctrinal conformity usually results in sectarianism. The process works like this. It is clear that we must "all speak the same thing" (1Cor. 1:10–KJV). However, since some teachings are more vital than others, we must determine which doctrines require agreement as a condition of unity.

In the absence of a hierarchy, we make this decision on the basis of careful Bible study. As church leaders study, write, and preach, a consensus evolves about the most important matters. Usually, this process involves a period of controversy. But in every consensus there are always dissenters. If they refuse to conform to the accepted interpretations, they are soon marked as false teachers because they have arrived at wrong answers on the issues. In reality, these issues are more determined by what seems to be important at the time than by what is at the heart of the gospel.[4]

Soon the true church is defined not only in terms of doctrinal fidelity to the Scriptures, but also on the basis of correctness on current issues. Those who disagree become "brothers in error"; in some cases, they may not even be regarded as Christians. The church is now perceived to be that body of people who agree upon a set of specific doctrinal issues which have been hammered out by a select few through discussion and controversy.[5]

Conformity has been attained and unity of the body achieved. But is this the unity for which Jesus prayed? Is this a unity based on relationship and love? Is it not rather a sectarian unity brought about by a human process? True unity is given to us in our relationship in Christ. It is not gained by pressing others into one's doctrinal mold.

Footnotes

1. The King James rendering misses the idea of the verse. The New American Standard reads, "Do two men walk together unless they have made an appointment?" The agreement is that of walking together, not of being in agreement in thinking.

2. Bryan Wilson, *Religious Sects: A Sociological Study* (New York: McGraw-Hill Book Co., 1970), p. 106.

3. The American Restoration Movement was greatly influenced in its method of biblical interpretation by John Locke and the Scottish Common Sense philosophers who advocated a rational approach to the Scriptures. Both Thomas and Alexander Campbell, who were most prominent in the theology of the movement, were under these British influences in North Ireland and Scotland before coming to the United States. The great emphasis on reason in Bible study stemming from this source has contributed to the call for conformity in externals. For an excellent study of influences in the movement, see C. Leonard Allen and Richard T. Hughes, *Discovering Our Roots: The Ancestry of Churches of Christ* (Abilene, TX: A.C.U. Press, 1988).

4. An example is seen in the discussion of whether the King James Version of the Bible is the only acceptable English translation. This could

hardly be an issue among Christians who speak other languages!

5. This process has been followed by many fellowships of believers. Each one concludes that it is the true church. The differences among them relate to the distinct doctrines that are regarded as essential to fellowship.

CHAPTER SEVEN

The Borders of the Kingdom

The Lord knows those who are his.
—Paul

It was June, 1968. John Ed Clark, newly-arrived American missionary to Ethiopia, was preaching at Gunjo in the district of Kambatta. About one hundred people had gathered to hear him speak in a newly-constructed, grass-covered tukal. In the audience was a stranger, unknown to anyone in the area. For two hours he listened as the preacher taught the word of God, and for another hour as he answered questions. Finally, the visitor stood up. He explained that he had come from the other side of the Omo River in Kaffa province, two days away by mule ride. He said that he and his people had heard that representatives of a church in America had come to Ethiopia. They understood that these people taught the Bible just as they did. He had come to see if this was true.

Conversation with the visitor revealed that he was the primary leader of a group of disciples who were simply following the teachings of the Bible. They numbered 1500 members in 51 congregations. For over forty years, they had not affiliated with any denomination. They called themselves "the church" and spoke of individual members simply as Christians. They immersed for the remission of sins. However, they did not observe the Lord's Supper weekly. Later visits to these people verified the representations made by their leader.

Were They Christians?

Based on this information, what was the spiritual status of this body of people. Were they Christians? If so, how should they have been regarded by other disciples of Christ? Did their failure to observe the Lord's Supper every Lord's day make them "brothers-in-error" from whom Christian fellowship should be withheld?

One's response to these questions is predicated on two assumptions: (1) that the information as related here is substantially correct,[1] and (2) that because of biblical precedent, it is important for Christians to partake of the Lord's Supper weekly. The second is called an assumption because, to many Protestants who do not accept the validity of the restoration principle, the frequency of taking the Lord's Supper is not particularly important.

Even some Restorationists are not convinced that the biblical evidence for eating the Lord's Supper every Lord's day is clear. At this point, our concern is not the correct frequency of observance of the Lord's Supper (though this is a valid question), but rather the significance of failing to observe it weekly, if in fact the Lord expects us to do so.

Before answering these questions, we should bear in mind that if an indigenous body, such as the one in Ethiopia, can come to a basically correct understanding of God's word without our assistance, this is also possible in our own communities. Our evaluation of the spiritual condition of the Ethiopian believers should be essentially the same if a similar indigenous movement were discovered in our own city. If this seems unlikely, we should remember that the American Restoration Movement was itself a coalescence of several "back-to-the-Bible" efforts. What occurred in Africa could also happen here.

Someone may object that because of personal convictions regarding the weekly observance of the Lord's Supper, he could not worship with these people if he were prevented from eating the memorial meal. That may well be true, but that is not the issue. I am asking, "Are these people Christians, and if so, what should be our attitude toward them?" My objective is for us to locate the borders of the kingdom of God.

To the ecumenically-minded person who is unconcerned about biblical authority, these questions will seem trivial. However, for those who embrace the restoration ideal as the proper means of learning the will of God, the questions are germane. They probe the heart on matters of conversion, fellowship, and Christian liberty. Our responses will also reflect our own sectarian perceptions, if such exist.

Possible Answers

Let us now consider several possible answers to the questions posed. First, some would deny that these people ever became Christians since they embraced error when they obeyed the gospel. This is not a straw man position. Several years ago, I served on a panel of four that dealt with matters of fellowship. After we gave our individual presentations, we fielded questions from the audience. One person asked how his congregation should respond to those from a noninstitutional congregation should they decide to cast their lot with them. How should they deal with their objections relating to certain types of congregational cooperation and their opposition to such institutions as children's homes? One of the panelists responded that it would be necessary to rebaptize these people because they had never become Christians. He based his conclusion on the oft-repeated premise, "You can't be taught wrong and be baptized right."

My fellow panelist was arguing that conversion to Christ requires more than a proper understanding of what is involved in the salvation process; it is also necessary that the candidate have a correct position on current doctrinal issues. I doubt that he would have pressed the matter so far as to demand conformity on every minor matter, but based on his reasoning, he certainly would have rejected the Ethiopians as children of God because of a flaw in their observance of the Lord's Supper. David Chadwell observes:

> Christians who are skeptical about the conversion of others still exist in the church. . . . These are the Christians who strongly feel there should be an approved indoctrination program before baptism. Understanding one's sinfulness, the atoning death of Jesus, the power of the resurrection, and the forgiveness of sin through His blood is not sufficient for baptism. People need to be taught all the "correct" doctrines and positions in the church first. Only if they understand and accept the "correct" positions are they ready for baptism.[2]

We should note that Philip the evangelist scarcely had time to brief the Ethiopian nobleman about the right answers to early brotherhood disputes before he baptized him. We are told, "Then Philip opened his mouth, and beginning with this scripture he told him the good news of Jesus" (Acts 8:35). To this message of salvation the queen's treasurer responded, "See, here is water! What is to prevent my being baptized?" (Acts 8:36). I do not suggest that Philip taught him nothing beyond the first principles of salvation from sin, but the context of the passage clearly indicates that his acceptance of Christ was unrelated to issues about which he was as yet totally uninformed.

A second response to our query about the status of the African disciples recognizes that their obedience to Christ made them Christians. However, their failure to observe the Lord's Supper weekly shows that they *believed* false teaching. Because this is a major error, it amounts to heresy. On that basis they are lost, outside the kingdom of God, and should be denied fellowship because of their erroneous faith.

This position can be illustrated in contemporary doctrinal issues. One of these relates to the nature of Christ's return. Will the second coming be premillennial? Some who oppose this view (and perhaps some who favor it) would define the boundaries of the kingdom on the basis of a correct theological understanding of the Lord's return. In other words, if one *believes* false teaching about the return of Christ, he should be denied the fellowship of other disciples.

Of course, it is true that some have become so enamored with their theories of the second advent that they have become divisive in promoting their interpretations. This is obviously wrong. Such a person should be subjected to the discipline of the church.

As for a man who is factious, after admonishing him once or twice, have nothing more to do with him, knowing that such a person is perverted and sinful; he is self-condemned. (Titus 3:10,11)

The spiritual shepherds must protect the sheep from those who would try to force their views on the church. However, discipline should not be administered because one *believes* an erroneous teaching, but because he has become *factional* in promoting his theology.

All of us unwittingly hold private views which are not in total agreement with God's word. Of course, it is possible for theological error to be so profound as to strike at the very heart of the Christian faith. John writes,

By this you know the Spirit of God: every spirit which confesses that Jesus Christ has come in the flesh is of God, and every spirit which does not confess Jesus is not of God. This is the spirit of antichrist. (1 John 4:2,3)

Because the kingdom of God is grounded in the deity of Jesus Christ, even a *belief* that denies this vital fact places one outside its realm. However, most doctrinal errors do not fall into this category, and the mere holding of an erroneous opinion on a doctrinal matter does not expel one from the kingdom.

We should remember that among the Corinthians whom Paul addresses as "the church of God . . . called to be saints" (1 Cor. 1:2) were disciples who denied the resurrection of the dead! (1 Cor. 15:12). Paul did not minimize the seriousness of the error. Rather, he dealt with it at length. On the other hand, he did not push those embracing this view outside the kingdom. They were still children of God, in spite of their flawed theology.

Still others evaluating the spiritual condition of the Ethiopian disciples would state that they should be regarded as "brothers-in-error" from whom fellowship should be withheld. They would readily grant that they became Christians when they obeyed the gospel. They would further state that a personal belief that weekly observance of the Lord's Supper is unnecessary does not place one outside the kingdom. However, by failing to follow the biblical example of taking the Lord's Supper every week, they have erred in practice. Their actions are sinful. Unless they repent of the sin, they are lost. Only a correction of their practice will restore them to the fold of God.

A problem with this position is that it requires repentance of those who are not conscious of having sinned. We are not dealing with willful sinners, but with those lacking the proper understanding of God's word. For one to confess that he has sinned when he does not believe that he has is hypocritical. Such a person is not being condemned for wrongful action (which he would correct if he knew better), but for his lack of knowledge. The crucial issue here is not the necessity of observing the Lord's Supper every week, but whether God will extend his grace to those who through ignorance err in their actions. If thorough knowledge becomes the basis of our salvation, then is there hope for any of us?

Those who define the borders of the kingdom on the basis of correct action more readily apply this yardstick in church affairs than in personal living. For example, the use of tobacco, which many Christians regard as sinful, is seldom cited as a reason to deny that one is a child of God. Rather, critical issues revolve around such tangible matters as correct worship, biblical organization, and the proper use of church funds. When division results over any of these issues, some will identify those congregations following "correct" action as "loyal churches"; those who disagree are, by implication, disloyal to the Lord and outside the kingdom of God.

The three attitudes we have considered have one thing in common. All define the borders of the kingdom in terms of acceptance and practice of correct doctrine. Though believers may initially have entered the body of Christ when they obeyed the gospel, those who in one way or another espouse doctrinal error are excluded from the kingdom on that basis.

The Role of Obedience

The rationale for this reasoning is based on the significance attached to obeying the commands of Christ. Many passages testify to the importance of obedience.

> *If you love me, you will keep my commandments.* (John 14:15)

> *If you keep my commandments, you will abide in my love, just as I have kept my Father's commandments and abide in his love.* (John 15:10)

> *By this we know that we love the children of God, when we love God and obey his commandments. For this is the love of God, that we keep his commandments.* (1 John 5:2-3)

Surely no thinking Christian would deny the importance of obeying our Lord.

On the other hand, do these verses, or any others that might be cited, imply that *perfect* obedience is necessary for our justification? Was not this the problem of the Pharisees? They insisted on perfect obedience down to the last spice, but none of them was able to achieve that objective. Therefore, Paul writes,

> *Then what becomes of our boasting? It is excluded. On what principle? On the*

> *principle of works? No, but on the principle of faith. For we hold that a man is justified by faith apart from works of law.* (Rom. 3:27,28)

The justification by works which the Jews sought was actually their effort to gain divine approval on the basis of perfect obedience. In this they were destined to fail. Thus, Paul demonstrates that it is by faith, not works of obedience, that one stands before God in righteousness.

It is apparent that when one determines loyalty to Christ on the basis of select doctrinal tenets, he begins to develop the party spirit. The doctrinal fragmentation of the Restoration Movement that results when one element repudiates another by asserting that it alone has the whole truth demonstrates how easily we fall into the sectarian trap.

The Undenominational Body

Our starting point as we seek to determine the borders of the kingdom must be Jesus Christ rather than fidelity to correct doctrine. The church is composed of those who have been saved from their sins by Christ. It is he who purchased the church with his blood (Acts 20:28). There is an identity between the spirit-filled disciple and the church. When one is saved, he is added by Christ to that body (Acts 2:47). Thus, the saved are in the church, and the unsaved are outside that fellowship. Thomas Warren puts it this way:

> In short, the Bible teaches that there are *no* Christians *outside* of the church for which Jesus died. When one obeys the gospel, being baptized (as a penitent believer) in the name of Christ (that is, by His authority), the Lord adds him to the church.[3]

Ultimately, the determination of those who are saved and within the kingdom belongs to the Lord: "The Lord knows those who are his" (2 Tim. 2:19). Unlike God, we are not omniscient. We cannot know a man's inner thoughts and must leave to the Almighty the judgment of the specific people whom he will save.

And what of the person who has truly accepted Jesus but lacks biblical understanding? How does he stand with God? Actually, this involves all of us, unless one is so bold as to affirm that he has a perfect understanding of every Bible teaching. Can one reach a point where he so departs from Christ as to leave his kingdom and be lost? Assuredly. The possibility of apostasy is clearly established in such passages as Hebrew 6:1-6 and 10:26,27. Certainly the rebel against God leaves his protective care. But how much error will God tolerate in our personal lives or in our understanding of his will? At what point do our actions separate us from the Father? Only he, who knows the human heart and makes his decisions on the basis of mercy and justice, can answer these questions. This I know! God is a God of grace, and if I am saved, it will not be because of my perfect obedience, but because of his grace in which I am redeemed in spite of my lack of knowledge or my imperfect actions.

The kingdom of God, then, encompasses all who through their acceptance of the gospel in the biblical way have been saved from their sins by the blood of Jesus. Some of God's children may so stray as to be lost, but only the Lord can determine those who have done so.

But can the undenominational body of Christ be exclusively identified with any fellowship of believers today? To put it another way, can we point to any group of Christians and affirm that they, and they alone, constitute the body of Christ? Some believe this is possible. Thomas Warren writes:

> I affirm–without the slightest fear of successful contradiction–that there are no Christians who are not members of the church of Christ.[4]

What does the writer mean by "members of the church of Christ"? Is he identifying the body of the saved as described in the New Testament? This certainly seems to be the case, and if so, there can be no disagreement with the statement.

However, most readers would assume that Warren is either designating these people in our day associated with congregations calling themselves churches of Christ, or that he is saying that the church of Christ of the first century is coextensive with the church of Christ of today, namely those congregations identifying themselves as churches of Christ and listed as such in the yellow pages of the telephone directory.

Whether or not this is one's position can be easily tested. Bible students are aware that the New Testament church is more frequently designated as "the church of God" than "the church of Christ" and that the terms are used interchangeably. Let us alter the statement to read, "I affirm that there are *no* Christians who are *not* members of the church of God." From a biblical perspective, such a change is appropriate. Is this statement correct? If one agrees that the revision is accurate, he clearly is thinking of the undenominational body mentioned in the Scriptures, that is, unless he is part of one of the denominations that calls itself the "Church of God." In doing so, however, he is also denying that modern-day congregations known as churches of Christ are the only people who are in the kingdom of God.

On the other hand, if one denies that the revised statement is accurate, perhaps because "the church of God" is a denomination, he is repudiating biblical language in order to identify those of a specific fellowship as being the only Christians.

The issue is not whether a group of disciples has the right to claim to be Christians only. Rather, it is whether those who are "Christians only" can justifiably profess to be the only Christians and that all others are thereby outside the borders of the kingdom of God.

The boundaries of the kingdom encompass all who have been born into the divine family, including the Ethiopian disciples. Only God can expunge their names from the Book of Life. For us to exclude them because we perceive some error in their thinking or practice is to be guilty of sectarian judgmentalism.

Footnotes

1. American missionaries visiting these people found a truly indigenous "Back-to-the-Bible" movement. An association begun with them was later curtailed by political developments in Ethiopia.

2. David W. Chadwell, *Beware of the Leaven of the Pharisees* (Abilene, TX: Quality Publications, 1985), p. 54.

3. Thomas B. Warren, *The Bible Only Makes Christians Only and the Only Christians* (Jonesboro, AR: National Christian Press, 1986), p. 148.

4. Ibid., p. 149.

CHAPTER EIGHT

The Key of Knowledge

Woe to you lawyers! for you have taken away the key of knowledge; you do not enter yourselves, and you hindered those who were entering.

—Jesus

Students of the gospels are familiar with the blistering denunciations which Jesus directed against the Pharisees. We sometimes overlook the fact that he leveled similar charges against the lawyers. Perhaps this was because many lawyers were also Pharisees (Matt. 22:35). Their appearance in the gospels is always associated with the Law of Moses rather than the Roman law, to which first-century Jews were also subject. Their major function was to interpret the religious law.

On one occasion, Jesus criticized the hypocrisy of the Pharisees (Luke 11:37-44). A lawyer in the crowd responded, "Teacher, in saying this you reproach us also" (Luke 11:45). Perhaps he expected that Jesus would exempt the legal profession from the charge. Instead, Jesus exposed the shortcomings of the lawyers by laying three woes on them. First, they loaded men with heavy burdens which they wouldn't help them carry. The burdens were the scribal interpretations of the Law (Luke 11:46). A second charge was the poor treatment they accorded the prophets. Though they gave the prophets lip service, they still acted like their forefathers who had slain them (Luke 11:47,48).

Jesus' third denunciation was, "Woe to you lawyers! for you have taken away *the key of knowledge*; you did not enter yourselves, and you hindered those who were entering" (Luke 11:52). *The key of knowledge* was the Word of God embodied in the Law of Moses, which the lawyers expertly interpreted. Jesus was saying that the lawyers did not fairly explore the implications of the law. Like some lawyers today, they were more concerned about the technicalities of the wording than in discovering the spirit that lay behind it. Even more serious was his charge that they stood in the way of honest searchers of truth. They not only misled the people, but also made sure that seekers of the Word could not learn its true meaning.

An Issue-Oriented Mentality

The lawyers and their Pharisee allies were issue-oriented nitpickers. Jesus clashed with them on how the Sabbath should be observed, the scrupulosity of their tithing, and the inconsistency of their oath-taking. They were so preoccupied with the details of correct observance of these things that they condemned all who disagreed with their application of the Law.

While it is easy to see flaws in these first-century Jewish teachers, we may not realize that sometimes Restorationists also have an issue-oriented mentality. A few years ago in a forum on "The Restoration Movement and Unity," I traced the history of religious issues in the twentieth century among a cappella churches of Christ:

> It is inevitable that, among people so deeply committed to truth as we are in the Restoration Movement, there should be doctrinal differences. This is not wrong. When others challenge our presuppositions and conclusions, we are forced to examine the legitimacy of our reasoning. However, we in the Restoration Movement have tended to seize on a few select issues and require that proper answers to those matters be given as a test of orthodoxy. Other matters, equally or more vital, are given little attention or are ignored. What we are concerned about are the "issues," as we call them.
>
> Consider some issues that have troubled us in this century. In the first

decade, the re-baptism question was fought hard and long, with the Mississippi River being the territorial dividing line. When someone from Tennessee went to Texas, he was immediately suspect because of where he came from. In succeeding years, there were lines drawn between North and South over Christian colleges, orphan homes, and opposition to located preachers. At the same time, and in other places, controversy raged over individual communion cups, simultaneous Bible classes, and women speaking in classes, not to mention disagreements over bobbed hair. . . .

The paramount controversy in the twenties and thirties was premillennialism. There had long been disagreement in the movement over the nature of the return of Christ, but no one had ever pushed the issue and peace prevailed. But when premillennialism became the issue, churches were split and brethren separated.

In the early forties, the main issue was whether a Christian could go to war. Discussion heated up almost to the point of division. Fortunately, the war ended before division came. Carnal warfare didn't seem to be so important in times of peace, and it ceased to be a divisive issue. But the change of time did not change the "rightness" or "wrongness" of a Christian's going to war. It was the issue, not the truth, that had changed.

The fifties brought us the questions of congregational cooperation, support of missionaries, and the renewal of the orphan-home issue; and then some began to debate about the legitimacy of eating in the church building and how the church building might be used otherwise. These were now the issues having replaced most of the earlier ones. As these matters died down, at least in some areas, the issues became the nature of the indwelling of the Holy Spirit, the King James Version versus other versions, and problems relating to marriage and divorce.

My point in enumerating this bit of history is to establish how issue-oriented we have been. We have determined soundness in the faith by the right answers to the right questions, but the issues continually change. Why don't we quarrel today about whether a disciple of Christ can go to war? Simply because this is no longer the issue. It will be if our nation ever goes to war again. The fact is, we do not know what questions will be used as a test of one's orthodoxy twenty years hence. I'm not, for one moment, suggesting that attention should not be given to critical problems which we face. Correct doctrine is important. But by the process of playing up some controversial issues when neglecting others, we have made people choose sides, which in turn has led to strained or broken fellowship. So long as unity requires conformity to correct belief in specific areas, our effort to achieve oneness will be severely impaired.

I think this illustrates how off-focus our message has often been. When we let Jesus be our focus, issues separating us somehow do not seem to be so divisive because we are looking at the One who is the author of our unity. We can begin to appreciate the principle of Christian liberty, in which the unity we have in Christ allows for some differences in understanding without our fellowship being affected. If today the soldier and the conscientious objector can sit side by side as they worship God, differing on what is now a "non-issue," can we not tolerate differences with one another in other matters? I do not believe that unity requires total agreement upon every issue. If that were the case, we would have to have a separate church for each one of us. Must I agree with you on how the Holy Spirit dwells within the child of God? Can we not be brethren

> even if you object to the English version of the Bible which I use? The fact is that we have made some issues more important than others. To those who contend the correct answers to half a dozen issues determine whether I am a faithful brother, what is the process by which you determine those beliefs which are essential to this relationship? How do you go about choosing which are "the issues" which must be the test of one's orthodoxy? My contention is that, in practice, the basis of that decision is what is currently being argued in our religious publications, rather than what is most important. We make our test of fellowship on a pick-and-choose basis and then heat up the issues in our lectureships to the point of division because we have now reached the state that communication and honest discussion of our differences becomes impossible.[1]

Removing the Key of Knowledge

When we seek to determine loyalty to Christ on the basis of "brotherhood" issues, we are taking away *the key of knowledge* from the average Christian. An inevitable consequence of an issue-oriented mentality is polarization, and this begets sectarianism. When issues are so heatedly argued that Christians are forced to choose sides, truth usually ceases to be the objective. If one refuses to line up with a certain position, he may by default be classified as belonging to the other side, even if he has no firm view on the matter. Usually "the issues" are pushed by religious publications, some of which were begun with the express purpose of promoting certain contemporary positions.

A few years ago, I received a phone call from a young man in the service inquiring about the congregation with which I was associated. He was looking for a "sound church" and was trying to determine if we met his criteria. His method of approaching the subject was to ask if I agreed with a certain religious magazine. I informed my caller that there isn't any magazine with which I totally agree, but as a matter of fact, I was in considerable disagreement with the magazine in question. Because of this response he concluded that the congregation of which I was a part was not a "sound" congregation.

The young man was most sincere and my comments are not designed to berate him. However, this incident does reveal how sectarian we can become. He was trying to determine our "soundness" by one or two current points of controversy. Had we measured up in those respects, we would have been a scriptural church in his eyes. Yet, what about the many, many other things which determine loyalty to Jesus? A congregation could be filled with hatred and materialism and yet, according to the young man's standards, be a "loyal, conservative" congregation.

Too long we have placed the yardstick on the superficial. Christians need to desist from evaluating congregations by their attitudes on specific issues. Perhaps the questions in debate are important, but to correctly evaluate, we need to examine the whole of a congregation–its worship, its doctrine, its attitudes, its dedication, its zeal to save lost souls. When we have done that, we will discover that every congregation falls short of perfection. This does not justify our imperfections, but we should be careful about passing judgment on others on the basis of a few correct answers to controversial questions.

What is the process by which *the key of knowledge* is taken away from God's people? Essentially, it involves marking and ostracizing those who do not toe the party line. Techniques that accomplish this purpose are common among those who have a great concern for doctrinal truth. In his book *In Search of Unity*, Edward Dobson, senior editor of *Fundamentalist Journal*, describes what he sees as excesses in the fundamentalist movement. Though restorationists are not technically fundamentalists, they do share with these people a high respect for the authority of the Scriptures. Therefore, some of Dobson's observations are relevant to this study.

Name-Calling

Dobson first mentions *name-calling*. He says that the more extreme fundamentalist separatist

> is always quick to call others by derogatory names such as *neo, pseudo, weak-kneed*, and *liberal*. Often this name-calling is a substitute for a clear and biblical examination of the issues that divide people. It is much easier to condemn than to cooperate. The most sweeping and devastating label is apostate. An *apostate*, by biblical definition, is a Christ-denier who has forsaken his profession of Christianity. (See 1 John 4:1-3.)[2]

To this catalog of names might be added *anti, compromiser*, and *modernist*. Once a name is attached to an influential person, it is repeated over and over in religious papers and public pronouncements until the person has been so stigmatized that others will not hear from his own lips what he believes. The next step is similarly to mark those who associate with him in person or who appear on the same program with him. The *key of knowledge* is removed from anyone who might be disposed to reexamine his biblical insights.

Paranoia

Dobson also writes about religious *paranoia*. He speaks of those who are perceived as being in positions of authority who see their influence threatened by others who are out to get them.

Dobson says:

> They nervously await every new book or magazine article as a threat to their very existence. Their vocabulary is filled with the language of warfare: *fight, contend, battle,* and *defend.* Their mode of operation is to "shoot first and ask questions later." Even when it is obvious they have overreacted, they refuse to apologize.[3]

Paranoia breeds a climate of fear. That fear may have no more basis than that it involves trying something new. In the forum previously mentioned on "The Restoration Movement and Unity," I observed:

> I am convinced that a major obstacle to unity efforts is fear. We are afraid that when some of us sit down with brethren with whom we differ, there will be compromise of the truth. We are afraid that when a new perspective of the word of God is presented, it may be heretical, simply because it is different. We are afraid that when a new idea is introduced, even though it is not wrong, it may lead to something wrong. We are afraid that if we stand up for what we believe is right, we may suffer personal loss. We have allowed a climate of fear to cause us to react rather than to act. It is

> time for each of us to have the courage to stand up for his convictions, rather than be intimidated by the criticisms of other brethren.[4]

Christians ought not to live in a spirit of fear. Paul says, "For you did not receive the spirit of slavery to fall back into fear, but you have received the spirit of sonship" (Rom. 8:15).

Isolation

Next, Dobson mentions *isolation* as a part of the marking process. He says that this technique stems from a sincere desire to achieve doctrinal and ecclesiastical purity, but results in "constant arguing and splitting."[5] The resulting polarization isolates Christians from one another. For example, speakers on lectureships may be limited to those who share the same perspective on a group of controversial issues. Naturally, those attending are of the same persuasion. Exposure to other views, which might give biblical insight on difficult questions, is not possible.

While such isolation may protect the unlearned from "dangerous doctrine," it also takes away *the key of knowledge*. As with the first-century lawyers who would not hear what Jesus had to say and prevented others from doing so as well, the doors of understanding are effectively closed to searchers of truth. They have been so isolated that they haven't even heard alternate interpretations.

It would be wonderful if truth were so neatly packaged that biblical interpretation would be unnecessary. Unfortunately, that is not the case. Every Bible teacher interprets the Scriptures, even the one who says that the Bible doesn't need interpretation! All explanations of biblical texts are interpretations. So long as this is true, we must make sure that a spirit of sectarianism does not remove *the key of knowledge* from those who seek.

Footnotes

1. Monroe E. Hawley, *The Restoration Movement and Unity* (Henderson, TN: Freed-Hardeman College, 1986), pp. 78-80.
2. Edward Dobson, *In Search of Unity* (Nashville, TN: Thomas Nelson Publishers, 1985), p. 74.
3. Ibid., p. 75.
4. Hawley, p. 136.
5. Dobson, p. 75.

CHAPTER NINE

Freedom in Christ

We are also persuaded that as no man can be judged for his brother, so no man can judge for his brother; every man must be allowed to judge for himself, as every man must bear his own judgment.

—Thomas Campbell

The Jewish church was in deep trouble. Some of its members were successfully persuading many of the faithful to accept the false teaching of a discredited rabbi. The rabbi had refused to conform to the accepted traditions of the church and had even denounced its leaders. The message he had taught undercut the creed of the church and, besides appealing to the riffraff, had taken in a few important people. Because the rabbi had threatened the security of the establishment, the Romans had crucified him.

Unfortunately, the death of the disgraced teacher only made him a martyr. Now some of his uneducated disciples were turning Jerusalem upside down by declaring that the rabbi had risen from the dead. Thousands believed them, and the church was split. Something had to be done, or the true Jewish faith would be in jeopardy. The only recourse was to warn the dissidents to stop preaching the message of the rabbi lest they be thrown into jail for creating a civil disturbance.

The leaders of the Jewish church had the two main heretical leaders arrested. They were uneducated fishermen named Peter and John. Sitting in council, the authorities warned them to stop talking about the former rabbi or face the consequences of their disruptive action. But to their surprise, the two followers of Jesus responded, "Whether it is right in the sight of God to listen to you rather than to God, you must judge; for we cannot but speak of what we have seen and heard" (Acts 4:19,20).

The apostles of Christ were undeterred by the intimidation. They went on preaching and once more were arrested and threatened with death. You see, they knew that even in prison they were *free in Christ*!

Freedom in Christ

In the state of Illinois there is a prison ministry called "Freedom Within." It says to the inmates, some of whom will be there for life, "Your body may be imprisoned, but no man can bind your soul if Christ has made you free."

A basic tenet of the Christian faith is that there is freedom in Christ. Consider some of the affirmations of the Scriptures. Jesus taught,

> *You will know the truth, and the truth will make you free.* (John 8:32)

Paul wrote,

> *For he who was called in the Lord as a slave is a freedman of the Lord.* (1 Cor. 7:22)

> *Now the Lord is the Spirit, and where the Spirit of the Lord is, there is freedom.* (2 Cor. 3:17)

> *For freedom Christ has set us free; stand fast therefore, and do not submit again to a yoke of slavery.* (Gal. 5:1)

Freedom From Sin

The concept that believers are free in Christ, even though physically limited, is called Christian liberty. It has broad implications. Freedom in Christ means freedom from the shackles of sin. Again Paul wrote,

> *But thanks be to God, that you who were once slaves of sin have become obedient*

> *from the heart to the standard of teaching to which you were committed, and, having been set free from sin, have become slaves of righteousness.* (Rom. 6:17,18)

A slave does not control his own life. The slave of sin is dominated by fleshly passions, often against his will. His life is out of control! But Jesus promises to liberate him from his bondage, freeing him from sin and the guilt that accompanies it.

Freedom From a Law-Mentality

Freedom in Christ is also freedom from a law-mentality. The New Testament epistles teach that Christians do not live under the Law of Moses, which gave spiritual direction to the first-century Jews. Paul wrote, "But now we are discharged from the law, dead to that which held us captive, so that we serve not under the old written code but in the new life of the Spirit" (Rom. 7:6). He also explained the significance of the death of Jesus as it related to the Law. "God . . . canceled the bond which stood against us with its legal demands [the Law of Moses]; this he set aside, nailing it to the cross" (Col. 2:14).

If the Law of Moses was omitted from the new Christian faith, so was the legal system of religion which it typified. The religion of Jesus is rooted in the human heart instead of deriving its strength from adherence to the letter. That is why Paul was concerned when he saw the Galatian disciples going back to the law approach as a means of getting right with God. Some Jewish Christians had disturbed these Gentile converts by insisting that a precondition of becoming a Christian was acceptance of the Mosaic rite of circumcision. Circumcision was not wrong in itself, but to require it as a condition of salvation was to effectively deny that sinners are saved by the grace of God. In that event, they would still be saved by a law system. Paul went so far as to declare that if they sought justification by the Law, they had already fallen from grace! (Gal. 5:4). He wrote:

> *Formerly, when you did not know God, you were in bondage to beings that by nature are no gods; but now that you have come to know God, or rather to be known by God, how can you turn back again to the weak and beggarly elemental spirits, whose slaves you want to be once more? You observe days, and months, and seasons, and years! I am afraid I have labored over you in vain.* (Gal. 4:8-11)

The observance of special days, months, and seasons was symptomatic. The Galatians thought God would accept them because they had earned salvation by keeping certain laws. They were actually being governed by human laws rather than divine principles.

Freedom to Think for Oneself

A third aspect of Christian liberty pertains to the right, and even the responsibility, of each Christian to think for himself. Paul teaches, "So each of us shall give account of himself to God" (Rom. 14:12). If I trust my soul to the direction of another person, I am depending on his wisdom for eternal life.

But Jesus also warns, "If a blind man leads a blind man, both will fall into a pit" (Matt. 15:14). Since all human beings make mistakes, it is perilous to follow the teachings of others without considering the validity of their views.

Many examples could be given of efforts to impose conformity of thinking among those following Jesus. The theology of the Roman Catholic Church, though not adhered to by all of its members, requires fidelity to the papacy. Ignatius Loyola, founder of The Society of Jesus, designed a list of rules for thinking with the church. Among them he directed the Jesuits:

> That we may be altogether of the same mind and in conformity with the church herself, if she shall have defined anything to be black which to our eyes appears to be white, we ought in like manner to pronounce it to be black.[1]

The extent of obedience to be given to the Pope was absolute:

> Let us with the utmost pains strain every nerve of our strength to exhibit this virtue of obedience, firstly to the Highest Pontiff, then to the Superiors of the Society; so that in all things, to which obedience can be extended with charity, we may be most ready to obey his voice, just as if it issued from Christ our Lord, . . . leaving any work, even a letter that we have begun and have not yet finished; by directing to this goal all our strength and intention in the Lord, that holy obedience may be made perfect in us in every respect, in performance, in will, in intellect; by submitting to whatever may be enjoined on us with great readiness, with spiritual joy and perseverance; by persuading ourselves that all things [commanded] are just; by rejecting with a kind of *blind obedience* (emphasis mine) all opposing opinion or judgement of our own; and that in all things which are ordained by the Superior where it cannot be clearly held that any kind of sin intervenes.[2]

Blind obedience! This is the mortar that has held the Roman Church together. Unfortunately, it allows little room for the individual to think for himself as it is based on the supposition that the church cannot be wrong.

But it is also possible for those professing to be just Christians to fall into the same trap. Consider the teaching in a church bulletin article entitled, "*Because I Say So*." The writer first cites Simon Peter's response to Jesus' command that they put out into deep water and let down their nets. Peter replied, "Master, we've worked hard all night and haven't caught anything. *But because you say so*, I will let down the nets" (Luke 5:5–NIV). The author of the article correctly observes that this reveals that Peter was a true disciple of Jesus because he took him at his word, even without understanding why. But the writer then applies this principle to the disciple who must also accept the word of his human teacher, even when he does not understand why. He states:

> Peter let down the nets not knowing what would happen because he trusted his teacher. *Do you trust those discipling you? Do you trust beyond the point of your own understanding*? . . . (emphasis mine) Do you fully obey when you're given direction and instruction or do you interpret, filter or revise what you hear? If we are really going to learn from others, we must decide to fully obey.[3]

Personally, I will obey Jesus blindly if he asks me to do so. This is because he is perfect and will not mislead me. But the article calls for new converts to follow blindly the direction of human teachers. The fallacy of this reasoning is that none of us is Jesus. We are all human beings, subject to human frailties and fallible understandings of God's word. I am unable to see any essential difference between the blind obedience imposed on the Jesuits and that cited in the article above. In one case, the Jesuit is to accept unquestionably the directives of the Pope; in the other, the Christian is to blindly submit to the one who is "discipling" him.

I do not want anyone to follow me blindly. When I teach others, I want them to come to a personal understanding so that their actions proceed from genuine conviction rather than "because I say so." Disciples of Jesus must be taught to think for themselves if they are going to answer for themselves in the judgment.

We should follow others only so far as we can see that they are following Jesus. Paul said, "Be imitators of me, as I am of Christ" (1 Cor. 11:1). It is fine to follow the good example of others–as they can help us much–but we must always look past them to Jesus, who is our teacher and perfect example.

If Christians are to be allowed to think for themselves, several things logically follow. Each person must be allowed to search out the meaning of the Scriptures. Others may assist by throwing light on the Word, but each one must ultimately determine what he believes it means. To do this, the individual must be free to question traditional interpretations without fear of reprisal. I have known of churches in which honest seekers were afraid to pose questions which, in the mind of the teacher, might betray an unorthodox understanding of a doctrinal issue. Merely to ask the question was to lay oneself open to being put down. But if we are truly searchers of the Word, we should be able to discuss any question that troubles the mind.

An example of this kind of intellectual intimidation is a three-page teacher's questionnaire used by the elders of a Texas church. After posing a number of queries relating to personal habits and attitudes, they ask sixteen doctrinal questions, most of which are currently being argued in religious papers. Though the elders do not explicitly state their own views, their perspectives are clear from the way the questions are phrased. Here are some examples: "Do you believe and teach that Christian women may *not* lead in prayer in classes or assemblies where men are present?" "Do you believe churches of Christ can cooperate with each other in supporting orphan homes and preaching the gospel?" "Do you believe and teach that a person who divorces for any other reason than adultery (fornication) and marries another person is living in sin?" "Do you believe and teach that the Lord's supper may be observed on any other day than the first day of the week?"

Now, I am fully aware that elders are responsible for seeing that truth is taught. I am also sure that I would agree with the views of these elders on most of the questions. Yet, I submit that a doctrinal questionnaire of this nature (which some feel amounts to a creed) intimidates the Christian who wishes to submit to the elders. He knows the answers the elders want, yet he is also aware that if he deviates from the "issue-line," he will be restricted in his ability to serve. There is no room in this climate for honest public disagreement and even little space for the holding of private opinions that deviate from those of the elders.

Freedom to Apply the Principles

Disciples of Christ must also be able to personally apply the principles of Christian living. The moral values of Jesus are fixed. Certain things are always right or wrong. Yet in the New Testament, most ethical teachings are stated in terms of principles rather than black or white commands. While the principle is clear, the application must be made by the individual. One is to love his neighbor (Luke 10:27), but exactly how this love should be demonstrated will depend on the situation. Christians are to dress modestly (1 Tim. 2:9,10), but modesty is determined partially by contemporary standards of society. At the beginning of the twentieth century a woman whose dress came a few inches below her knees was considered immodest. Such is not true today. Later, churches debated the propriety of bobbed hair. More recently, Christians have disagreed about the modesty of a woman wearing pantsuits or slacks in public worship.

These are obviously debatable issues. Ultimately, the individual must personally determine what is acceptable to God as he applies the principles of Scripture.

Dangers of Christian Liberty

There are some dangers in thinking for oneself. Some fear that new Christians will arrive at wrong conclusions and that they must, therefore, be protected from going down the wrong path. Of course, any new convert can make mistakes just as a teenager given the right to make a decision may choose unwisely. In teaching their young people to live in an adult world, most parents expect teenagers to make choices that the parents want. But the freedom to choose carries with it the possibility of bad choices. However, unless our children are given the right to choose, they will be unable to function in a world without parental guidance. I recently observed a pair of cardinals feeding their young one by placing the seed directly in his beak. But as I write this, I see the juvenile feeding himself. The parents did not continue to feed him because he would never learn to feed himself unless he was given the opportunity.

So it is with the young convert. We can provide him with what we believe are correct answers, but he cannot indefinitely remain a babe in Christ. He must learn to feed himself, and this he can do only when he has learned to think for himself.

A more serious problem occurs when Christians are not taught to think for themselves. A new generation will grow up with all the right answers, but without convictions. A person may affirm that it is wrong to engage in certain activities without understanding why these activities are wrong.

Those who advocate thought-control fear honest investigation of truth. But why should one be afraid? Truth has nothing to fear when exposed to honest examination!

Moreover, Christians who are not taught to think for themselves will be unable to cope with false teaching when it does appear. They are like Jehovah's Witnesses who can read the answers to new questions from a book, but are totally incompetent to respond to questions for which their book gives no answers. What frequently happens is that the one who has learned the answers by rote realizes that he cannot defend his faith. Too often he ends up abandoning his faith altogether. I suspect that were a survey made of young people who have lost their faith, we would discover that many had never learned to personally decide the critical issues of life.

The Restraints of Freedom

If Christian liberty gives one the privilege of thinking for himself, Christian love also imposes restraints on that liberty. One's freedom in Christ must never become a stumbling block to others. The early church struggled with the propriety of eating meat that, after being offered to idols, was then sold in the marketplace. In this, Paul warned that it is more important to act responsibly in love toward one's brother than to exercise his Christian liberty.

> *If your brother is being injured by what you eat, you are no longer walking in love. Do not let what you eat cause the ruin of one for whom Christ died. So do not let your good be spoken of as evil.* (Romans 14:15,16–RSV Harper Study Bible)

Paul was saying that while eating certain foods is permissible, it becomes wrong when one's action causes another to stumble spiritually.

> *And so by your knowledge this weak man is destroyed, the brother for whom Christ died. Thus, sinning against your brethren and wounding their conscience when it is weak, you sin against Christ. Therefore, if food is a cause of my brother's falling, I will never eat meat, lest I cause my brother to fall.* (1 Cor. 8:11-13)

Faith and Opinion

A vital issue involving spiritual liberty relates to doctrinal differences affecting the fellowship of Christians. Thomas Campbell sought to solve the problem by rephrasing an often-repeated motto to read, "In matters of faith, unity; in matters of opinion, liberty; in all things, love." Campbell knew that there are vital matters upon which Christians must agree. These are matters of faith. Some other things, he believed, relate to opinion and should not disrupt Christian fellowship. The problem with Campbell's motto is that it does not provide a means of distinguishing faith and opinion. In doctrinal controversy, one element will identify an issue as being a matter of faith, while the other side places it in the realm of opinion. In practice, the one on the theological right often places issues under the heading of faith while the one on the left identifies them as opinion.

A study of Romans 14:1-15:7, in which both faith and opinion are discussed, is vital to an understanding of Christian liberty in personal relationships. A part of the passage reads:

> *As for the man who is weak in faith, welcome him, but not for disputes over opinions. One believes he may eat anything, while the weak man eats only vegetables. Let not him who eats despise him who abstains, and let not him who abstains pass judgment on him who eats; for God has welcomed him. Who are you to pass judgment on the servant of another? It is before his own master that he stands or falls. And he will be upheld, for the Master is able to make him stand. One man esteems one day as better than another, while another man esteems all days alike. Let every one be fully convinced in his own mind. He who observes*

> *the day, observes it in honor of the Lord. He also who eats, eats in honor of the Lord, since he gives thanks to God. . . . Why do you pass judgment on your brother? Or you, why do you despise your brother? For we shall all stand before the judgment seat of God. . . . Welcome one another, therefore, as Christ has welcomed you, for the glory of God.* (Rom. 14:1-6,10,15:7)

An examination of this passage shows that the faith being considered is the personal faith of the individual rather than the body of Christian teachings sometimes called "the faith." The New International Version renders verse 1, "Accept him whose faith is weak" and in the next verse states that "one man's faith allows him to eat everything." Then in verse 23 Paul adds, "But he who has doubts is condemned, if he eats, because he does not act from faith; for whatever does not proceed from faith is sin." So Paul is speaking of the faith of the individual disciple rather than the truth revealed in the Scriptures.

Next, Paul mentions disputes over opinions. He proceeds to discuss two debatable issues–eating meats and observing special days. Was he classifying these issues as faith or opinion? T. William Daniel clarifies the matter:

> Paul was not speaking about matters that were either "faith" or "opinion." Rather, he speaks of things that are both

> "faith" and "opinion!" These were matters of conflicting *"opinions,"* each of which arose from *"faith."* "One man's faith allows him to eat everything, but another man, whose faith is weak, eats only vegetables" (v.2). . . . And the word "opinion," as many of our translations have it, is a lot more inclusive than we might like to believe. It means "thought," "opinion," "reasoning," or "design." My opinion is what I think. Some of my opinions are based upon strong proof. Others are not. Either way, it is still what I believe, my opinion.[4]

And what does Paul say should be our attitude toward those of diverse opinions?

> *Accept him whose faith is weak, without passing judgment on disputable matters.* (Rom. 14:1–NIV)

> *Accept one another, then, just as Christ accepted you, in order to bring praise to God.* (Rom. 15:7–NIV)

Disputable matters! These are the doctrinal issues that trouble us. Paul makes it clear that I must accept my brother who disagrees with me in matters of opinion. I really have no option if I am to be true to God's word. I must accept my brother because Christ has first accepted me and him.

But what were these things of which Paul spoke? One related to eating meat. There were some who believed it was sinful to eat meat that had been offered to idols and then sold in the marketplace. Paul did not believe this was wrong unless by eating such meat another person was made to stumble (1 Cor. 8:7-13). Some apparently went so far as to become vegetarians. Paul describes such a person as a weak brother, but makes it clear that both vegetarians and meat-eaters must accept one another.

The other issue pertained to the observance of special days. Some regarded all days as equally important. Others, perhaps those of Jewish culture, would elevate such special feast days as the Passover or Pentecost above ordinary days. Paul told the Romans that each opinion must be respected and that neither party should put the other down. A modern counterpart of this is whether such days as Christmas and Easter should receive special treatment. Were Paul with us today he would respond in the same way: "Let every one be fully convinced in his own mind" (Rom. 14:5).

Paul goes so far in his treatise as to direct Christians to stop judging one another.

> *Why do you pass judgment on your brother? Or you, why do you despise your brother? For we shall all stand before the judgment seat of God; . . . So each of us shall give account of himself to God. Then let us no more pass judgment on*

> *one another, but rather decide never to put a stumbling-block or hindrance in the way of a brother.* (Rom. 14:10,12,13)

Paul reasons that since each one is directly responsible to God for his actions, we have no right to get into the judging business simply because we hold different views.

But were these issues peripheral or were they doctrinal matters that go to the heart of the Christian faith? Michael Armour shows that they did indeed relate to crucial doctrinal questions:

> But some may object that Paul is talking only of ethnic and social diversity, not of what we would call "doctrinal" diversity. Stood alongside the New Testament, however, these objections do not bear the weight of examination. Most of us would consider the matter of honoring "holy days" to be doctrinal in nature. But Paul said our unity can embrace men of totally opposing views as to whether such observances are proper (Romans 14:5).
>
> That same chapter offers still another example of "doctrinal diversity" which is even more striking. I refer to the controversy about meat sacrificed to the idols. Since the problem of eating such meat does not present itself to us today, we tend to hurry through the passages in

Romans 14 and 1 Corinthians 8 which address the issue. In that hurry-through perhaps we have not given these chapters the serious reflection they deserve.

I presume that we all understand the specific problem which triggered Paul's counsel about meats. But to the disputants, the underlying issue was not eating meat. The real issue was what constitutes worship and service of idols.

Now, nothing was more characteristic of the early church than its staunch opposition to idolatry. The council at Jerusalem placed only four restrictions on Gentile converts, and atop the list was separation from anything offered to idols (Acts 15:29). The book of Revelation thunders the warning that Christians must pay any price–including death–to avoid compromise with idolatry. Along similar lines, Paul insisted that the Corinthians "flee from idolatry" (1 Corinthians 10:14). He was equally insistent that they not think they could "partake of the table of the Lord" while continuing to participate in the table fellowship of pagan deities (1 Corinthians 10:20,21). Indeed, historians frequently identify the most characteristic features of the early church as her abhorrence of idolatry, her high standards of sexual purity, and her commitment to charitable works.

Thus, a question about what constitutes the worship and service of idols was hardly a marginal issue. To the first century Christian no matter was more urgent than disassociating himself from pagan religion. The man who abstained from eating any meat, lest it be tainted with idolatry, could argue that his practice, while extreme, was nonetheless the safest and most prudent course for Christians. After all, if idolatry is damnable, one must keep himself as far from it as possible.

Another, however, insisted that he could sit in an idol's temple, eating meat in the very shadow of the statue itself, without incurring the guilt of worshipping or serving a pagan deity (1 Corinthians 8:10). How could two views be more opposed to one another–and on a matter so crucial as the Christian's relationship to paganism! Yet Paul dismissed neither of these men from the Christian circle. There was room in the congregations at Rome and Corinth for vegetarian and meat-eater alike.

Imagine what we have here: two Christians attending the same congregation, one of them believing that what the other does on a weekly if not daily basis betrays the very essence of Christianity. Even flirting with idolatry, he feels, strikes at the very heart of the doctrine

> that there is but one God. Yet Paul tells this man, "Don't condemn your brother." And to the man who feels free to eat meat he says, "Don't look with contempt on the man who disagrees with you" (Romans 14:3).
>
> If Christian unity can spread its arms around such diverse viewpoints on a subject so vital as avoidance of idols, surely it can embrace those on both sides of the "issues" which have derailed the restoration effort.[5]

Though it should now be apparent that in this passage the issues were doctrinal, we should remember that Paul puts them in the realm of opinion (Rom. 14:1). Apparently, strong beliefs about doctrinal matters can be classified as opinions because they involve personal interpretation of the Scriptures. Opinions can be right or wrong. They should not be relegated to the realm of the inconsequential. Some opinions can cause us to be lost. But this is not Paul's point. He is saying that the Lord is our judge, and in the meantime, we are obligated to accept as brothers those with whom we disagree in doctrinal matters, even if we believe them to be dead wrong. He does not say that we should not discuss our differences and, if they relate to important things, seek to persuade others of the truth we find in God's word. But even so, if they have truly accepted the gospel of Christ, we must acknowledge them as brothers.

A study of Paul's letter to the Romans should convince us that there is more latitude for disagreement among Christians than we may realize. It is natural for those grounded in the necessity of having a "thus saith the Lord" for their beliefs and actions to feel that those who interpret certain Scriptures differently are endangering their souls by such convictions. We must be aware that it is the Lord who will judge them. In the meantime, we must learn to accept them as fellow disciples in Christ.

The principle of Christian liberty, so strongly taught in the epistles, was one of the foundation-stones of the Restoration Movement. In the preamble of Thomas Campbell's historic "Declaration and Address," Campbell clearly advocated this ideal.

> We are also persuaded that as no man can be judged for his brother, so no man can judge for his brother; every man must be allowed to judge for himself, as every man must bear his own judgment–must give account of himself to God. We are also of opinion that as the Divine word is equally binding upon all, so all lie under an equal obligation to be bound by it, and it alone; and not by any human interpretation of it; and that, therefore, no man has a right to judge his brother, except in so far as he manifestly violates the express letter of the law. That every such judgment is an

> express violation of the law of Christ, a daring usurpation of his throne, and a gross intrusion upon the rights and liberties of his subjects.[6]

Let those who are the spiritual heirs of this great reformer hold to the biblical ideal which he so clearly expressed. By so doing, we will do much to rid ourselves of the sectarian spirit.

Footnotes

1. Ignatius Loyola, "Spiritual Exercises," part 2, *Documents of the Christian Church*, ed. Henry Bettenson (Oxford: London, 1967), p. 260.
2. Ignatius Loyola, "Const. vi.I: Mirbt, 431," *Documents of the Christian Church*, ed. Henry Bettenson (Oxford: London, 1967), p. 261.
3. Ed Townsend, "Because You Say So," *Boston Church of Christ Bulletin*, August 17, 1986.
4. T. William Daniel, "'Faith' or 'Opinion'–Is That the Question?" *IMAGE*, April 15, 1987, pp. 13,14.
5. Michael Armour, "The Nature of Unity," *Restoration Forum V* (Joplin, MO: College Press, 1987) p. 141,142.
6. Thomas Campbell, "Declaration and Address," *Historical Documents Advocating Christian Union*, ed. C.A. Young (Chicago: Christian Century, 1904), p. 72.

CHAPTER TEN

Symptoms of Sectarianism

Crystallization of custom has been the germinating power of sectarianism.
—Wendell Broom

Every person periodically visits his doctor for the treatment of illness. Invariably, the doctor asks a series of probing questions: "Where do you hurt?"; "How long have you felt this way?"; "Is it getting worse?"; "Have you been running a fever?"

The questions posed by the doctor relate to symptoms. Each answer may shed some light on the physical problem causing the ailment. The physician is not primarily concerned with the symptoms, but he must identify them to determine their cause.

The malady of sectarianism also has symptoms which warn of a spiritual problem. There are several reasons why the symptoms must be identified and taken seriously. First, they focus on a spiritual condition needing correction. We usually learn about our physical ailments from the symptoms–a headache, a pain in the chest, or an upset stomach. A person can take an aspirin for the headache to relieve the symptom, but an aspirin will not cure a serious problem. The medication attacks the symptom rather than the infection. Still, it is important to heed the symptom's warning. Likewise, taking note of sectarian symptoms can help correct the sectarianism.

Second, sectarian symptoms are serious because of their negative effect on those searching for truth. Honest seekers are turned off by the plea to be just Christians when those who make this profession do not practice what they preach. A major obstacle to successful evangelism is the sectarianism which seekers observe in the actions and attitudes of their would-be teachers. I know a fine man, formerly a pastor in a major denomination, who was distressed by the spiritual lethargy and lack of biblical base of his church. He began a search for a congregation after the scriptural order. Though there was such a body in his small community, he did not even consider it in his quest because of the dogmatism he had seen in a relative who was a member of a sister-congregation in another state.

Third, sectarian symptoms occasionally devastate sincere Christians who are repulsed by bad attitudes in their home churches. People have despairingly sought my counsel after encountering such a negative spiritual emphasis. The problem almost always related to some expression of sectarianism. Today, many people are rightfully concerned about the loss of young people to the cause of Christ. Although some of it can be chalked up to the infidelity to which they have been exposed in college or to poor peer associations, we cannot overlook the adverse effect of the sectarian spirit they see in their home congregations. Failure to recognize this as a problem is to bury our heads in the sand.

Sectarian Speech

During the judgeship of Jephthah, following the Israelite conquest of Canaan, a civil war erupted among the tribes on opposite sides of the Jordan River. The people of Gilead took the fords of the Jordan to guard against the enemy. Whenever one from the other side sought to cross the river, he was given a simple test to determine his loyalty. If he denied being from Ephraim, he was asked to say "shibboleth." If he pronounced the word "sibboleth" instead, he was immediately killed because his accent revealed him to be an enemy (Judg. 12:1-6).

Our speech often betrays us. When Simon Peter denied that he was one of Jesus' disciples as the Master was being tried, the bystanders said, "Surely you are one of them; for the way you talk gives you away" (Matt. 26:73–NASB). Just as Peter's accent betrayed him, so one's profession of being undenominational will fall on deaf ears if he or she speaks sectarian language.

An example of sectarian speech is the common misuse of the term “church of Christ.” The words simply identify the body for which Jesus died as Christ’s church. It is a descriptive expression as are other biblical terms such as “church of God,” “the body of Christ,” “the kingdom,” and “the way.” None of these is a proper name. In fact, there is no proper name in the New Testament that collectively identifies biblical congregations.

To employ any biblical term to the virtual exclusion of others is to use a scriptural expression in a sectarian way. To speak of “church of Christ doctrine,” “church of Christ preachers,” “church of Christ members,” “church of Christ schools,” and even “church of Christ churches,” reveals a sectarian mind-set just as surely as if one spoke of “Baptist doctrine,” “Baptist preachers,” “Baptist members,” “Baptist schools,” or “Baptist churches.” The message conveyed by such speech is that “we are a sect or denomination like the Baptists, Methodists, or Lutherans.” Though one may deny that this is the case, that is the way the message is usually read. A plea to be just a Christian seems hollow when the language says otherwise.

How should we express ourselves if our speech is to match our profession? Instead of “church of Christ doctrine,” why not say Bible? Instead of “church of Christ members,” why not speak of Christians? Instead of “church of Christ preachers,” why not use biblical language to identify gospel preachers?

It is not improper to use any scriptural term, such as "church of Christ," if we do so biblically. We do not do this when we use it *exclusively* to describe the Lord's spiritual body.[1]

Traditionalism

Traditionalism is another sectarian symptom. We are all captives of our culture and our time-honored customs. Both culture and tradition add stability to our lives. Religious traditions may significantly contribute to the cohesiveness of the church. After all, traditions are merely accepted ways of doing things. A problem arises, though, when traditions become so entrenched that they are perceived as law. Wendell Broom observes that "crystallization of custom has been the germinating power of sectarianism."[2]

A few years ago, a sister in a new congregation–a friend of many years–asked my evaluation of that work. As she was obviously upset, I inquired about her concern. She responded, "Well, that church just isn't us." I asked her to be more specific. She replied, "They don't call themselves the church of Christ and they don't sing an invitation song." So far as she was concerned the church was apostate.

Her problem was not that the new congregation was unbiblical, but that it had breached tradition. It chose to be known to the community simply as "the church" rather than "the church of Christ." Since "the church" is the most frequent New

Testament designation of the Lord's body, how can this be wrong? As to the invitation song, it is a carryover from the revivalistic days of the nineteenth century.[3] This does not make its use either wrong or unwise. It is simply a traditional expedient to give people an opportunity to obey the gospel. But my friend saw something else in her concerns. She believed God's will had been forsaken when only tradition had been changed.

Countless illustrations of the entrenchment of tradition can be given. I know of churches that have dispensed with Sunday evening services to divide into small groups for fellowship. Some regard this as abandoning the truth, when in reality, nothing is said in the Scriptures about the necessity of meeting twice on Sunday. The use of a church building owned by a congregation is normative in our society and in most cases is expedient. Yet the early disciples met in houses and halls. Aside from the logistical problems created by the physical limitations, what is improper about our doing the same thing? After all, many existing congregations met in homes until they could secure more commodious facilities. However, in some cases if this were done, some people would "quit the church" because they could not function without a permanent building in which to worship.

A problem with traditionalism arises when it is insisted that procedural matters be carried out uniformly. To ono unfamiliar with the traditions involved, this makes a law where God has not made one. The truth-seeker may turn elsewhere if he sees that tradition has replaced the Word of God.

Dogmatism

"You can't tell him anything. He has all the answers!" How often have you heard that statement about another person? This is the dogmatist who is never wrong–even when confronted by the evidence. Somehow he feels that it is a sign of weakness to admit that he has made a mistake or changed his mind.

One dictionary defines "dogmatism" as "unfounded positiveness in matters of opinion; arrogant assertion of opinions as truths."[4] Most of us are affronted by the dogmatic person when he pontificates in politics or economics. Religiously, dogmatism is especially offensive when one's attitude conflicts with the spirit of Jesus.

Note that the dictionary identifies arrogance in the dogmatist. This is apparent when he asserts that he can't be wrong. Still, it is unfair to assume that all dogmatic people are arrogant in the abrasive sense. Some folks are simply so sure that they are right that they kindly assert that they aren't wrong and that closes the matter. This is the quiet kind of dogmatism.

> Religious dogmatism often relates to one's inability to distinguish between what the Bible says and his explanation

> of it. To the dogmatist his interpretation is identical to the actual words of the scriptures. If another rejects his interpretation he accuses him of denying the authority of God's word. Now, if a passage has been correctly translated, we can be sure that we are reading the words from God's Holy Spirit. But the moment we say, "This is what it means," we have injected our own understanding. Interpretation is essential, but it is important to realize that one's personal understanding could be wrong. The dogmatist often cannot distinguish shades of gray. Everything is simple–black or white. But that is not the way it is. The biblical teaching may be clear, but the situation to which it must be applied may be highly complicated and not one to which a quick and simple answer can be given.[5]

The dogmatic religious person is always highly sectarian. His inability to see another point of view is repugnant to truth-seekers who want to be treated as intelligent individuals. Some folks who are not dogmatic by nature display dogmatic religious attitudes because they can't understand how they might be wrong. What we must realize is that one's strong personal conviction should never cause him to put down those with whom he disagrees.

Judgmentalism

Finally, judgmental attitudes are symptomatic of a sectarian spirit. Restorationists correctly point out that God has not given man the right to change his commands. We cannot legislate for the Lord by writing creeds or delivering official interpretations of the Bible. God is the lawgiver rather than we. By the same token, it is not our prerogative to get into the judging business for God, since he alone is the judge.

Jude relates the otherwise biblically unrecorded encounter of the archangel Michael with Satan in a dispute over the body of Moses. We know nothing more about this than that Michael "did not presume to pronounce a reviling judgment upon him, but said, 'The Lord rebuke you'" (Jude 9). If God's archangel dared not do God's judging against the devil, neither have we the right to assume God's position to condemn our fellowman.

It is judgmentalism to tell another person that he is going straight to hell if he does not comply with a specific divine command. The judgment may be correct, but no one has the right to try to do God's work for him. Paul makes this clear when he writes the Romans, "Who are you to pass judgment on the servant of another? It is before his own master that he stands or falls" (Rom. 14:4).

The judgmental spirit stems from a legalistic approach to the Christian faith which allows God no leeway in his dealings with man. From this perspective God must apply his divine laws rigidly, and since we think we can correctly interpret them, we have the obligation to warn others of what God will do with them eternally. However, this approach does not reckon with the grace of God. If grace means anything at all, is there not the possibility that because of his merciful nature and complete knowledge, God may in some situations forgive those who fall short of the mark? None of us knows the limits of divine grace, and hence, we cannot commit God to a specific course of action.

Does this mean that we should not warn sinners of the consequences of their behavior? Not at all. The Christian has the responsibility to teach the Word. If the Word teaches that "all liars . . . shall be in the lake that burns with fire and brimstone, which is the second death" (Rev. 21:8), we must teach that truth. If Jesus declares that "he who believes and is baptized will be saved; but he who does not believe will be condemned" (Mark 16:16), we have an obligation to teach that truth. If one hears the Word taught in the proper spirit and rejects it, he is condemned by the Word, not by the teacher. But if the teacher goes beyond this to pronounce a personal judgment on the one being taught, he has exceeded his role as a teacher.

In summary, inaccurate terminology, traditionalism, dogmatism, and judgmentalism are all symptomatic of sectarianism and when present should warn one of a spiritual problem. Though not the problem itself, these things adversely affect others both in and out of Christ. Each Christian has the responsibility to identify his problem and to correct it.

Footnotes

1. For a more detailed study of sectarian speech, see Monroe E. Hawley, *Redigging the Wells* (Abilene, TX: Quality Publications, 1976), pp. 83-94.

2. Wendell Broom, Sr., *The Crystallization of Custom* (Abilene, TX: Abilene Christian College, no date), p. 6.

3. Thomas H. Olbricht, "The Invitation: A Historical Survey," *Restoration Quarterly*, vol. 5, no. 1, 1961, pp. 6-16.

4. *The Random House College Dictionary* (Random House, 1975).

5. Monroe E. Hawley, *The Focus of Our Faith* (Nashville, TN: 20th Century Christian, 1985), pp. 105, 106.

CHAPTER ELEVEN

The Life of Grace

A Christian is so far perfect as not to commit sin.

—John Wesley

As a young preacher, I once presented a sermon I called "The Ladder to Heaven," designed to show how we are saved by grace. I put some ladders on the blackboard illustrating how some people hope to reach the eternal home. The first four ladders I identified as "man's way" because they incorrectly represent the journey between earth and heaven. I called them "good works only," "good conscience only," "faith only," and "grace only." Then I drew a ladder depicting "God's way." It began with obedient faith, subdivided into primary obedience and secondary obedience or works. The top of the ladder I labeled grace. My purpose was to show that after we have obediently done our part, God's grace makes up what we lack.

The sermon fell short in that it did not set forth the whole truth about grace. The Bible says, "For by grace you have been saved through faith; and this is not your own doing, it is the gift of God–not because of works, lest any man should boast" (Eph. 2:8,9). You see, we are not saved partially, but *totally* by grace. Grace doesn't just enter into that part of our lives in which we fall short. We don't earn part of it by obeying the gospel and another part by doing good works. All of our salvation, Paul says, is by grace.

I am not the only one to have had this misconception of grace. Rubel Shelly tells of a preacher who responded to the question, "What do you understand grace to be?" by replying, "Grace is doing all you can of the will of God–maybe 90 percent or 95 percent–and God taking up the slack."[1] Shelly then added:

> People who do not see themselves as recipients of divine grace cannot practice grace with one another. Thus there will be suspicion, fear, and isolation.[2]

I would not suggest that most Christians do not believe in grace. On the contrary, I am confident that virtually all Bible believers, certainly all restorationists, accept the concept of grace. One cannot restore New Testament Christianity without teaching grace. Our difficulty is that we may not fully appreciate the role of grace in our lives. This, in turn, distorts our faith.

Neither is the inclusion of a chapter on grace in a book about sectarianism meant to suggest that a misunderstanding on this subject necessarily makes one sectarian. Certainly it does not. However, there are some erroneous views of grace which provide the basis for sectarian attitudes. It is to these that we will give special attention.

Moral Perfectionism

A study of historic holiness movements reveals that many of them have subscribed to a theory of spiritual perfectionism. This was true of the early Methodists who accepted the theology of John Wesley. Wesley taught that "a Christian is so far perfect as not to commit sin."[3] The American Holiness Movement adapted Wesley's views to teach that by a personal experience the Christian is sanctified with a "second blessing" to reach perfection. The perfectionism of the holiness movement was reflected in its austere moral values which not only opposed dancing and drunkenness, but also fine dress, sabbath-breaking, and card-playing.

American restorationists have rejected Wesley's theory of perfectionism, but in some instances have developed their own perfectionist theology. This is true in the moral realm. An example is the teaching which insists that there must be specific repentance for each sin committed. Leslie Diestelkamp writes:

> Of course each and every sin offends God. He hates them all! But some are saying that each and every sin destroys our *relationship* with God. One writer said, "My brother, one sin will separate you from God. . . . Forgiveness is available to the Christian upon the condition that he will confess that sin to God." Notice "that sin." (From *Guardian of Truth*, Aug. 13, 1981). Another writer said, "No passage in all the Bible teaches that any sin ever was, or ever will be, forgiven prior to repentance of THAT SIN. In every example that God inspired and preserved for our learning, specific repentance antidates forgiveness." Notice the phrases, "THAT SIN" (his emphasis) and "specific repentance." (From *Searching the Scriptures*, p. 13, the date unknown to me–perhaps in the early '80's).[4]

This idea that each sin must be specifically repented of can be illustrated by drawing a horizontal line with the area above it labeled "safe" and the area below titled "lost." Before conversion the sinner is in the lost area. When he obeys the gospel he crosses into safe territory. When he commits a sin after conversion, he immediately drops below the line and is lost. When he confesses that specific sin and asks God's forgiveness he again crosses the line into the safe area, that is, until he again sins, and the process is repeated. Thus, the Christian journey is a roller coaster, alternating between lost and safe. We would hope that one would die when he is above the line. Unless he does, he cannot be saved by the grace of God!

Or suppose that a man driving down the highway thinks an evil thought. Perhaps he even verbalizes his feeling with an oath. Just then, his car is struck by a train and he is instantly killed–all before he can confess to God, "Lord, I have sinned, please forgive me." Does he have no hope?

The ramifications of this theory are frightening. The follower of Jesus can never be sure where he stands with his Lord. Is he safe or lost? Spiritual security is an impossibility. What if one has committed a sin which he has forgotten? He can't ask God's forgiveness because he doesn't recall his sin. Unless he can "say the secret word" he is destined to remain below the line and be lost–forever! And what about his unconscious sins? Surely all of us are guilty of sins of ignorance. We can't repent of what we do not know. Or what of those things we have done that were in the gray area? We frankly don't know if they were sinful.

This perception of sin inevitably leads to a life of guilt. The Christian with an overactive conscience is tormented by the fear that he might have unconsciously sinned or that he might have failed to ask forgiveness. He becomes so preoccupied with sin that he finds no joy in the Christian walk and always fears that he hasn't done enough. In time he may cry out, "Lord, it is more than I can bear," and turn his back on his Savior, all because he has not learned the significance of the grace of God.

Living in Grace

These misconceptions of God's grace result from a failure to understand that grace is a state rather than an isolated act to be called forth at our request. To illustrate, Paul and Barnabas urged their followers *"to continue in the grace of God"* (Acts 13:43). Paul declares that through Christ "we have obtained access to this *grace in which we stand*" (Rom. 5:2). He continues,

> *Where sin increased, grace abounded all the more, so that, as sin reigned in death,* grace also might reign through righteousness *to eternal life through Jesus Christ our Lord.* (Rom. 5:20,21)

Peter says that we should *"grow in the grace* and knowledge of our Lord and Savior Jesus Christ" (2 Pet. 3:18).

These passages show that the Christian lives in a state of grace. As long as he is faithful to the one who died for him, he can have assurance that he is in a safe spiritual condition. He lives a life of grace. Grace becomes God's power to help him be spiritually triumphant. When Paul petitioned the Lord to remove his thorn in the flesh, the divine response was, "My grace is sufficient for you, for my power is made perfect in weakness" (2 Cor. 12:9). In other words, as long as Paul was living in the state of grace, the Lord would give him the strength he needed to meet his problems.

All of this relates to God's forgiveness of the sins of his children. John writes,

> *My little children, I am writing this to you so that you may not sin; but if any one does sin, we have an advocate with the Father, Jesus Christ the righteous; and he is the expiation for our sins, and not for ours only but also for the sins of the whole world.* (1 John 2:1,2)

This assurance of forgiveness applies to conscious sins we commit through weakness and to willful sins when we repent of them. But does this promise also apply to sins of ignorance and sins we may commit before we can ask forgiveness? If indeed, grace is a state and if we are living in that condition, our forgiveness should be assured. Fortunately, the Scriptures address this problem. Paul writes,

> *So also David pronounces a blessing upon the man to whom God reckons righteousness apart from works: "Blessed are those whose iniquities are forgiven, and whose sins are covered;* blessed is the man against whom the Lord will not reckon his sin." (Rom. 4:6-8)

This simply means that God forgives the Christian who sins through ignorance because he is living in grace. It also means that the one hit by the train before he could ask forgiveness is forgiven–because he is in Christ where grace is found. Thus, the faithful Christian, with John, may know that he has eternal life (1 John 5:13).

This assurance that we have in Christ produces a different mentality from that of the one who lives in constant fear that he may do something wrong. When I was a boy, there was a saying often repeated by children on the sidewalk: "Step on a crack and you'll break your mother's back." Some children believed it was true and carefully avoided every crack. Children of God don't need to walk in the spiritual path with that kind of apprehension because we live in the grace of God.

Doctrinal Perfectionism

Some in the Restoration Movement take the perfectionist ideal into the doctrinal realm. This relates to the role played by obedience in attaining God's grace. David Chadwell compares the attitudes of the Pharisees with those of some contemporary restorationists:

> The crux of the confrontation is quite evident: what role does obedience play in making one righteous? Pharisaism said obedience played the primary role. The Pharisees did not regard themselves as

legalists in this issue. They believed in the essentiality of God's grace. Aside from Jesus' identity as the Christ, the issue was this: does obedience appropriate the grace of God or does faith appropriate the grace of God?

In this matter the parallel between the Pharisaic view and the view held by many New Testament Christians is chilling. Be it understood (1) that no faction of the restoration church today regards themselves as being legalists, and (2) that all factions would openly declare they believe in the essentiality of God's grace. However, many believe and strongly affirm that a New Testament Christian is righteous and justified before God because (1) he is a member of the restoration church, and (2) he is doing approved works. It is the act of obeying the right teachings that makes a member of Christ's church righteous. Righteousness is not the result of a divine act in human life made possible by proper faith, but the result of collective human acts in honoring the church's teachings and approved way of doing religious acts.

There continues to be a confrontation between factions over the question of how a person can stand as righteous in God's eyes. The crux of the confrontation

> remains the same: what role does obedience play in making one righteous? The issue remains the same: does obedience appropriate the grace of God, or does faith appropriate the grace of God?[5]

Biblically speaking it is clear that we are justified by faith. "For we hold that a man is justified by faith apart from works of law" (Rom. 3:28). "Therefore, since we are justified by faith, we have peace with God through our Lord Jesus Christ" (Rom. 5:1). This simply means that God accepts us on account of our faith in Christ.

The faith that saves is not mere mental assent to Bible truths, but is a personal trust in Jesus. As such it is necessarily obedient. Paul speaks of "the obedience to the faith" (Rom. 1:5; 16:26). Obedience is not distinct from faith, but is an integral part of it! We dare not downplay its importance because of its role in the faith saving process.

However, this is not what Chadwell is considering when he speaks of those who seek God's grace by means of obedience. He is talking about the idea that unless Christians perfectly obey certain commands, they forfeit the right to eternal life. Norman Bales describes an encounter with a critic who cited James 2:10 from the King James, "For whosoever shall keep the whole law and yet offend in one point, he is guilty of all." He followed the quotation with his personal conclusion, "Now, remember preacher, if we fall short on just one little point, we've disobeyed God entirely."[6]

The critic missed James' thought. James was not saying that perfect obedience is essential to salvation; rather, he was demonstrating that no one is sinless and that all fall short. It is precisely on that account that we all need the grace of God or we would be without hope.

Realistically, no one can call for perfect obedience on every minor point. Since no two people are in total doctrinal accord, it is apparent that perfect agreement is impossible. What some do call for is doctrinal perfection on certain prescribed issues. If one is wrong in these doctrinal actions, he is sinning; and as long as he continues to do so, he is lost.

Concerning the Ethiopian disciples mentioned in an earlier chapter, some will reason that their failure to observe the Lord's Supper weekly was doctrinally sinful. Unless they would correct their practice, they would be lost. This is the reasoning that seeks to appropriate God's grace on the basis of obedience rather than by faith.

The insistence that those who unwittingly continue in certain doctrinal errors are condemned to eternal punishment disregards the nature of repentance. If one sins by intent, he is a rebel against God and has no hope without repentance. This applies both morally and doctrinally. However, repentance involves a change in heart which in turn requires a proper understanding of truth. You cannot repent of gambling until you learn that it is wrong to gamble. You cannot repent of failing to observe the Lord's Supper until you have learned that you are violating the divine will. It may be objected that once a person is told that his action is wrong, he becomes disobedient when he fails to comply with the correction he has received. However, merely to tell a person that he should observe the Lord's Supper every Sunday may not convince him even if the point is crystal clear in the mind of the one proposing the correction. Though I personally believe gambling is wrong, I have discovered that some honest, sincere Christians don't buy all of my arguments, simply because there is no specific command that says, "You shall not gamble." One does not become a rebel against God because he disagrees with my conclusions (even if my deductions are correct) and persists in his course of action. He does become a rebel when he is convinced by God's word that he is wrong and fails to take corrective action. "Whoever knows what is right to do and fails to do it, for him it is sin" (James 4:17).

There are many Christians who err doctrinally because they have not understood some truth or correctly applied some biblical principle. The same grace that forgives when we morally fall short due to ignorance covers us when we miss the mark doctrinally by the same ignorance.

How does one's inability to grasp the breadth of God's grace pertain to sectarianism? In this way: As it has been shown, a limited view of grace causes one to be unsure of his salvation. If I am not confident that God will overlook my sins of ignorance or the conscious sins for which I do not specifically ask forgiveness, I am not going to look favorably on others who fall short by my standards. If I feel that in every important area God requires perfect obedience, I am driven to the conclusion that there is little hope for those who lack in such critical areas as worship. Therefore, I believe it is my responsibility to warn them to repent and to inform them that unless they change their ways, they will be lost.

This is judgmentalism at its worst. Judgmentalism is an expression of sectarianism. Many of us can recite horror stories of someone who has rejected the plea for apostolic Christianity because he talked with a person who informed him that he was going straight to hell if he didn't change his practices. Doubtless the one making the pronouncement thought he was acting in the best interest of the other person, but all he did was to convince him that "those folks have a holier-than-thou" attitude.

We all crave security. This is especially true spiritually. We want to know that when we die we have an eternal home awaiting us. For some people, that assurance is based on the conviction that if they are doctrinally right they are approved of God. They have found that position with which they are comfortable. They are not interested in further exploring God's word to find new truths because such a discovery may require change. Change threatens security. The very idea that one might be wrong is disquieting to the one who rests his salvation on doctrinal correctness.

An appreciation of the breadth of God's grace liberates us from this uncertainty. Because we have been saved by grace through faith, rather than by doctrinal accuracy, we may be assured that we stand in the proper relationship with our Father.

Perhaps part of our problem is that we do not know God well enough. If we did, we would realize that as a God of mercy, he desires that we live lives of grace.

Footnotes

1. Rubel Shelly, *The Restoration Movement and Unity* (Henderson, TN: Freed-Hardeman College, 1986), p. 102.
2. Ibid., p. 102.
3. R. Newton Flew, *The Idea of Perfection in Christian Theology* (Oxford: University Press, 1968), p. 326.
4. Leslie Diestelkamp, *Think On These Things*, vol. 18, no. 1, p. 1.
5. David W. Chadwell, *Beware of the Leaven of the Pharisees* (Abilene, TX: Quality Publications, 1985), pp. 58, 59.
6. Norman L. Bales, *How Do I Know I'm Saved*? (Nashville, TN: Christian Communications, 1989), p. 99.

CHAPTER TWELVE

Anatomy of a Division

It takes a sectarian to ferret out a sectarian, just as "it takes a rogue to catch a rogue."

—David Lipscomb

One of the rarest human talents is the ability to view oneself objectively, or, as Bobby Burns would put it, "to see ourselves as others see us." Many who can quickly discover flaws in other people have difficulty in seeing their own deficiencies. This is true of some Christians who can easily detect sectarianism in other folks, but are unaware that they suffer from the same malady. David Lipscomb once observed, "It takes a sectarian to ferret out a sectarian, just as 'it takes a rogue to catch a rogue.'"[1]

Because personal objectivity is hard to learn, it helps to examine the struggles of others in order to appreciate our own. For that reason, we shall look at the struggle with sectarianism of a particular body in the restoration tradition.

The Brethren

The Brethren Movement originated in the British Isles in the early nineteenth century. Others called these people the Plymouth Brethren because one of their largest and most influential assemblies was in Plymouth, England. They speak of themselves simply as "Brethren" or "Christian Brethren," and have consistently repudiated the designation of Plymouth Brethren. We shall simply call them the Brethren.[2]

There are many similarities between the Brethren and the Restoration Movement. Both have roots in eighteenth- and nineteenth-century British restorationism. The influence of James and Robert Haldane, for example, is a common factor. Both movements began about the same time. Both adopted the restoration approach to Christianity. Both placed great emphasis upon biblical authority and rejected all human creeds. Both strenuously opposed sectarianism in any form. Both rejected denominational terms as valid designations of the body of Christ, the Brethren even more so than those associated with the Campbells and Stone. Both practiced congregationalism and repudiated any intercongregational authority. Both emphasized baptism and the weekly observance of the Lord's Supper. And both called for unity, but wrestled with division. The 1936 United States religious census listed eight distinct bodies of Brethren, and that does not exhaust the factions.[3] Of course, there are also differences between the movements which might suggest that paralleling the two efforts is inappropriate. However, they have so much in common that it is desirable to consider what happened to the Brethren as a means of analyzing the sectarian problem in the Restoration Movement. Discussion of their difficulties is not designed to remove the splinter from another's eye while having a log in one's own, but is rather intended to be a mirror by which restorationists of our day can examine the sectarian process.

The Brethren Movement resulted from the consolidation of several independent religious efforts in Britain in the 1820s. Its foremost leader was John Nelson Darby, whose influence among the Brethren was as pervasive as that of Alexander Campbell in the American movement. Darby was a man of great ability who devoted his life to evangelism. He was highly respected among the Brethren, and his ideology profoundly affected both his proponents and antagonists. He was given to speculation about future things and is generally regarded as the father of dispensationalism. By his strong will and untiring zeal, he placed his stamp so strongly on the movement that outsiders dubbed it "Darbyism."

Division Rears Its Head

Another noted leader was Benjamin Wills Newton, the most prominent teacher of the seven hundred member congregation in Plymouth. Newton had been greatly influenced by Darby, but this changed when Newton became convinced that Darby's theology caused him to teach that there are two schemes of salvation. At Plymouth he opposed this teaching publicly. When Darby arrived in Plymouth for a visit in March, 1845, for the purpose of vindicating his views, conflict was assured. Darby began his own teaching sessions to counteract Newton's influence. After considerable infighting, Darby concluded that it was fruitless to stay with the church on Ebrington Street. He withdrew from the congregation and split it by drawing away members who began assembling at another location.

A couple of observations are in order. Darby, by virtue of his strong personality, had a devoted group of followers who were willing to follow blindly wherever he led. A common element in the development of sectarianism is the devotion of people to a leader more than to Jesus. In this instance, as in most cases of doctrinal turbulence, the difficulties were not rooted so much in issues as in the dogmatic personalities involved. The division between Darby and Newton was more personal than doctrinal. As time was to tell, the personality clash was the underlying factor in the first major division in the Brethren Movement.

Darby had another characteristic which greatly contributed to the schism among the Brethren. He had a genuine fear of heresy, which prompted him to be continually on the alert for any vestige of false doctrine. Though it may be an overstatement to describe him as a heresy hunter, it was true that he would harshly condemn anyone who opposed him. He could not appreciate the possibility that he might be wrong. Roy Coad comments:

> Once again that curious strain in Darby's make-up appears: his inability to stand in the place of the other man, and his assurance that anything which opposed his own work was *ipso facto* born of evil.[4]

This kind of mentality cannot distinguish between what the Scriptures say and one's interpretation of the Word and provides the soil in which the seed of sectarianism germinates.

The Plymouth situation worsened as charges and counter charges were hurled. Darby's continuing barrage had the effect of isolating Newton and his congregation from many of the Brethren. Still, he didn't quite have what he needed to fully destroy Newton. Then, in 1847 it fell into his hands–the notes of a sermon Newton had presented two years earlier as taken down by a listener. In his message Newton expressed some views regarding the sufferings of Christ which caused some of the Brethren to question his orthodoxy. To us the issue would seem like a tempest in the proverbial teapot, but for Darby it was proof positive that Newton was a heretic and must be marked as such. Rather than personally contact Newton to verify the accuracy of the notes, he rushed into print to condemn him. Here was a clear expression of sectarianism–a spirit of unfairness that would resort to almost any tactic to accomplish its objective.

The verbal and printed onslaught against Newton by Darby and his partisans caused Newton to reevaluate his thinking regarding his teaching. In November, 1847, he published a retraction. That should have ended the matter, but it did not. Newton left the Ebrington Street church after his retraction, and the congregation issued its own repudiation of the doctrine in question. That also should have ended the dispute, but by this time the deep-seated sectarian spirit had so enveloped Darby and his associates that they would not drop the matter.

Sometime thereafter, two members of the Plymouth congregation visited Bethesda chapel in Bristol. This was a flourishing assembly with outstanding leadership that had done its best to stay aloof from the controversy. The visitors were questioned as to their views of the position attributed to Newton which he had now repudiated. They assured the Bethesda leaders that they did not accept these ideas and were accordingly received without further discussion. Word of this action reached Darby's ears. So far as he was concerned, not only was the Plymouth assembly heretical, but so was Bethesda chapel because it harbored heretics. That meant that Bethesda also accepted the false doctrine! Bethesda expressly rejected the alleged erroneous teaching, but this was not acceptable to Darby. He and his circle of churches proceeded to mark Bethesda as well.

You might think that would have ended the matter. It did not, as the cancer spread even farther. Darby discovered that some churches in Yorkshire were sympathetic to Bethesda. Alarmed, he then insisted that those who sympathized with Bethesda should also be marked. Broadbent explains how far the excommunicating process was carried:

> Even Darby's marvelous influence could not impose this great change on all, but, by untiring propaganda, a large number of churches were induced to accept as a necessary test of fellowship the condemnation of the church at Bethesda on account of a doctrine never held by it. By dint of constant repetition this circle of churches came to believe, in all sincerity, that Bethesda had been cut off for holding Newton's error, an error which he himself had repudiated, and which the church at Bethesda had never entertained. So consistently was this system carried out that Negro brethren in the West Indies had to judge the

> Bethesda question, and Swiss peasants in their Alpine villages were obliged to examine the errors attributed to Newton and condemn them.
>
> Such a system could not fail to lead to further divisions. Even in Darby's lifetime, several such took place, the parties taking different sides excluding each other as rigorously as they had unitedly excluded Groves and Muller.[5]

Within the space of five years, the Brethren movement was irreparably divided. In succeeding decades the "exclusive" Darbyites continued to divide and subdivide. A major factor underlying the divisions of 1879, 1884, 1890, and 1908 related to where lines of fellowship ought to be drawn as each splinter became increasingly more restrictive. The "open" or "independent" churches, repudiated by the Darbyites, have replaced the "exclusives" in numerical superiority, and, though holding a wide range of views, have for the most part remained united.[6]

A Study in Sectarianism

Having examined the events surrounding the sad division among the Brethren, let us now consider how sectarianism played a part in the scenario. A key element was partisanship stemming from the following of human leaders, especially Darby. The real issue of the dispute was not, "What is truth?" but "Whose side are you on?" Doctrinal issues were a subterfuge for a power struggle. This is so far removed from the spirit of Jesus that there is no way it can be defended.

Coupled with the party spirit was political coercion. A fuller examination of the whole story reveals conferences and publications designed to whip wavering churches into line. Those who refused to go along with the collective decisions were threatened and marked until they came around to the "correct" position. An atmosphere of intimidation prevailed.

There was a phobia about heresy. Charges were made and statements distorted. Even those who unequivocally repudiated Newton's position were charged with holding his views. So entrenched was the fear of error enveloping the Brethren that basic fairness and honesty were forgotten.

Congregational autonomy was consistently violated as prominent church leaders applied pressure to make wavering assemblies conform. This occurred among people who had rejected the hierarchical system in favor of pure congregationalism. But congregationalism is not always a safeguard against power politics which demands conformity to the party line.

Some of those involved in the struggle were committed to disunity. The division was marked by an absence of genuine efforts to resolve the problem. Commitment to disunity is a commitment to sectarianism. Separation cannot always be avoided and occasionally may even be necessary, but we must never forget that division displeases God. Christians, therefore, must be committed to work for the unity of God's people, even in the face of disunity.

Finally, the whole process was fraught with judgmentalism. Even if it is granted that Newton was in error and that his congregation should not have allowed this doctrine to be taught, it is sad to note that when he disavowed his teaching, his accusers rejected his retraction. When the Plymouth assembly renounced his error, they were not accepted back into the fold. The others were simply unwilling to listen.

Then there was the Bethesda assembly. The congregation never accepted Newton's views. They were so conservative that they would not even accept those from Plymouth until they had been quizzed about their theology. Yet Bethesda was marked because it had accepted individuals who denied the doctrine in question, all of this after both Newton and the Plymouth assembly had made the same denial!

Sectarianism had gone to seed, but not to the extent that it would later. Finally, other churches, never charged with accepting Newton's teaching, were excommunicated because they would not draw the line against Bethesda which had never accepted his views in the first place. A potential question was whether fellowship could be extended to those who rejected the Bethesda assembly, but accepted those churches that accepted Bethesda.

The question was not asked because by that time the movement was totally divided.

Many of us have encountered some of these sectarian attitudes and actions in one way or another. I personally had such an experience. In the early 1950s I twice edited a directory of churches in the northern part of the United States. We decided not to omit congregations based on doctrinal differences. We felt that the individuals using the directory should make their own determination as to the soundness of any congregation listed. Some disagreed with that policy and I respected their position. A personal friend became quite upset with the policy and wrote the publisher explaining his reasoning. Then he added, "I have written Bro. Monroe Hawley all the above and much more. I cannot fellowship him or anyone who does fellowship him until he makes clear that he has repented of the wrong he has committed."

We were never able to resolve our differences, but that is not nearly so significant as the statement of this brother that he would not fellowship anyone who fellowshipped me. What about the person who wouldn't fellowship me but would fellowship the person who does? Would he extend his recognition to such an individual? Carried to its logical conclusion, my friend would have found himself fellowshipping only his wife, and maybe not even her!

Finally, sectarianism is a problem with which all Christians must struggle. The tragedy is that too often we cannot see it in ourselves. It is likely that Darby never realized that he had a sectarian spirit. After all, he himself had left the established church to become nonsectarian. But a claim to be nonsectarian is invalid unless it is acted out. Let us, then, use the tragic story of division among the Brethren to illuminate our own shortcomings. May that mirror help us individually to practice the undenominational Christianity of which we read in the Word of God.

Footnotes

1. David Lipscomb, "Sectarians In the Worship," *Gospel Advocate*, April 25, 1907, p. 265.

2. An excellent history of the Brethren is given by F. Roy Coad in *History of the Brethren Movement* (Grand Rapids: Wm. B. Eerdmans Publishing Co., 1968). The details of the matters discussed in this chapter are found on pages 105-163.

3. *Religious Bodies: 1936* (Washington: U. S. Government Printing Office, 1941), vol. 2, pp. 291-327.

4. Coad, pp. 133, 134.

5. E. H. Broadbent, *The Pilgrim Church* (London: Pickering and Inglis, 1955), pp. 384, 385.

6. The present status of the "open" assemblies is described by the well known scholar and member of the Brethren, F. F. Bruce, in *In Retrospect* (Grand Rapids, MI: Wm. B. Eerdmans Publishing Co., 1980), pp. 282-290, 313-317.

CHAPTER THIRTEEN

Focusing on Jesus

Sir, we would see Jesus.
—Some Greeks visiting Jerusalem

In one of the lesser known stories in the gospels, John tells about some Greeks who approached Philip asking to see Jesus. Since they had gone to Jerusalem for the Passover, they were probably "God-fearers." These were Gentiles who accepted the ethical superiority of Judaism, but were unwilling to embrace its ceremonial rituals. Cornelius was a God-fearer (Acts 10:1,2) as were many other early Gentile converts (Acts 17:4).

We are not told why the Greeks went to Philip. They simply said, "*Sir, we would see Jesus*" (John 12:21–ASV). After Philip discussed the request with Andrew, they took it to Jesus. Whether Jesus gave them an audience, we are not told.

Our interest in this story centers on the request to see Jesus. Is seeing Jesus not what the Christian faith is all about? If we cannot see Jesus in the flesh like the Greeks did, we must "see" him in a spiritual sense if we are to understand the essence of his teachings. Moreover, as disciples seeking to bring others to the Great Teacher, we must be certain that it is *Jesus himself* that we help them see.

The apostles and early Christian teachers saw the person and mission of Jesus as the heart of their faith. They did not just teach facts about Jesus, but spoke of him as one with whom they enjoyed a personal relationship. Their message focused on Jesus; everything else was secondary. Paul declared,

> *When I came to you, brethren, I did not come proclaiming to you the testimony of God in lofty words or wisdom. For I decided to know nothing among you except Jesus Christ and him crucified.*
> (1 Cor. 2:1,2)

The Christological nature of the apostolic proclamation is reinforced by reading the sermons recorded in the Acts of the Apostles. A study of seven of these reveals that though each presentation was tailored to the audience, the ultimate message always centered on Christ. Other passages tell us, "And

> every day in the temple and at home they did not cease *teaching and preaching Jesus as the Christ*" (Acts 5:42). "Then Philip opened his mouth, and beginning with this scripture *he told him the good news of Jesus*" (Acts 8:35). "Others said, 'He seems to be a preacher of foreign divinities'–because *he preached Jesus and the resurrection*" (Acts 17:18).[1]

The epistles are permeated with language picturing the total union of the disciple with Jesus. For example, in Colossians 2:12-3:4, Paul seven times uses the term "with Christ" or its equivalent. The follower of Christ is said to die with him, to be buried with him, to be raised with him, to be made alive with him, to have his life hidden with him, and ultimately to appear with him in glory.

Over and over again we are informed that Christians are "in Christ." Paul uses the expression thirteen times in Ephesians 1. This is the theme of Romans 6 which establishes the complete identification of each believer with Jesus. In Colossians 1:27 Paul reverses the image by stating that the mystery of God "is Christ in you, the hope of glory."

The centrality of Jesus in the biblical message ought to be evident to every student of the Scriptures. Strangely, even committed disciples of Christ sometimes do not grasp this fundamental truth. A few years ago a preacher of the gospel was criticized by a fine Christian couple for the content of his preaching. When he asked them to be specific, they replied, "You preach too much about Jesus and love."

Why did these people complain that there was too much preaching about Jesus? They were committed Christians. They were also well educated. What they really wanted was a diet of first principles. As long as the core of the teaching was Christ, they did not feel that these first principles were being properly stressed. They did not realize that there are no principles so fundamental as Jesus and love.

But is it really possible to preach too much about Jesus? If one objects that by preaching Jesus some themes will be neglected, he overlooks the fact that other topics are relevant only so long as they pertain to Jesus. If one preaches Christ, he will also preach about repentance and baptism. We know, for example, that after Philip preached Jesus to the Ethiopian eunuch, the nobleman requested baptism (Acts 8:35,36). Neither can one proclaim Christ without also emphasizing the role of the Lord's Supper in our commitment to him. One cannot even correctly stress the elements of godly living without preaching Christ, for the essence of living for Jesus is being like him. The person of Jesus becomes the controlling factor in our thinking, "for the love of Christ controls us, because we are convinced that one has died for all" (2 Cor. 5:14).

How does this relate to our theme of sectarianism? It is simply that those with the sectarian spirit rarely focus on Jesus. This is not to say that they may not reverence him or preach about him. Rather, they do not make Jesus the focal point of their spiritual attention. As we have observed, an issue-oriented theology often accompanies the sectarian spirit. When one is preoccupied with religious issues, his attention ceases to be riveted on the Lord.

We can quickly recognize that the Pharisees were classical sectarians. We must also remember that they devoted themselves to a correct understanding of God's word. They spent countless hours reasoning about the details of the Sabbath, sacrifices, and tithing in order to please God. *But they could not see Jesus*. They became so enamored with the written word that they lost sight of the Living Word! Jesus told them, "You search the scriptures, because you think that in them you have eternal life; and it is they that bear witness to me; *yet you refuse to come to me that you may have life*" (John 5:39,40).

We, too, must be certain that instead of focusing on the details of the written word, and perhaps not seeing Jesus, we center our attention on the Living Word as viewed through the Scriptures. This does not diminish one iota the authority or importance of the Bible as God's revelation. Quite the opposite: we value it for its illumination of our Savior rather than looking at it only for itself. We can stare so hard at the window as we peer into the house that we do not see the person it frames.

Necessity of Balance

As we analyze the subject, it becomes evident that *sectarianism is distortion*. Distortion results from improper emphasis. Ira North's book, *Balance*, is based on the thesis that lasting church growth requires balance in the total congregational program.[2] He is correct. Improper emphasis on a single facet of the work of the church impedes ultimate church growth. Even evangelism, if stressed at the expense of grounding converts in their new faith, will bring only short-term results.

Focusing on Jesus provides the necessary balance to correct sectarian distortions. This can be illustrated by considering some of the sectarian problems we have examined.

Doctrinal Emphasis

The doctrine of the first-century Pharisees was woefully out of balance. They focused on external actions, but neglected the spiritual aspects of justice, mercy, and faith (Matt. 23:23). They were not wrong in keeping the letter of the law; they were wrong in neglecting the spiritual dimension.

Those grounded in restoration tradition correctly stress the importance of following God's word. However, this can result in overemphasizing controversial issues so that the larger picture of the Christian faith is neglected. An issue-oriented mentality inevitably causes sectarianism, not because truth is not taught, but because it is distorted.

Jesus is our corrective. When we make him *the focus of our faith*, doctrinal disagreements will not be ignored, but they will be discussed in view of their relevance to Christ, in the spirit of love which Jesus enjoins on his followers. Discussion will not be designed just to win converts to a position (and hence to polarize), but to provide a basis for a mutual understanding growing out of our common faith in Jesus.

Biblical Interpretation

Restorationists are vitally concerned about correctly understanding and applying the Scriptures. To do this, however, the written word must be interpreted. Comparison of historic restoration efforts across the centuries shows that diverse answers have often been given to difficult questions. These may stem from different systems of interpretation. The Bible must not only be accepted as authoritative, but it must also be correctly interpreted.

It is not our intent to explore the conflicting approaches that men have used to search out biblical truth. However, the weakness of many of these systems is that they are based on methods which do not put Jesus in focus. He must be our starting point. Restoration interpretation tends to focus on *effect* material rather than *cause* material.

Preaching centers more in Acts (the effect) than in the gospels (the cause). However, before one can properly understand the early church as described in Acts, he must come to know Jesus as portrayed in the gospels.

If we ground our Bible interpretation in Jesus, we will seek to discover his mind-set. As we wrestle with ethical questions, we will find ourselves asking, "How would Jesus respond?" In disputes about doctrinal issues we will inquire, "How does this relate to Jesus, his teaching, and his plan of salvation?" Truth will not be discovered simply by appealing to close reasoning; rather our reasoning will grow out of its relation to Christ.

Making our biblical interpretation focus on Jesus will not immediately resolve all differences. However, in most instances, we will restore balance to discussion and negate the sectarian polarization which results from failing to give Jesus his proper place in our dialogue.

Unity With Other Believers

The restoration ideal cannot be fully implemented apart from a commitment to work for unity among God's children. Such a commitment does not guarantee that oneness will be achieved. Impediments may involve the restrictions of one's conscience or the unwillingness of others to join the search for unity. But where the commitment is present, there is always hope that it can eventually be realized.

Division often results from improper emphasis on the details of the Christian faith as distinguished from the core message centered in Christ. Conversely, the road to unity must be found by restoring the proper balance to the faith as it focuses on Jesus.

Too often it is presumed that all truth is equally important and, therefore, that for unity to exist there must be agreement on the details of all truth. This is not correct. Paul wrote,

> *For I delivered to you* as of first importance *what I also received, that Christ died for our sins in accordance with the scriptures, that he was buried, that he was raised on the third day in accordance with the scriptures, and that he appeared to Cephas, then to the twelve.*
> (1 Cor. 15:3-5)

The good news of the death, burial, and resurrection of Jesus is *more important* than how often we eat the Lord's Supper or how churches can biblically cooperate. This does not make these things inconsequential, but rather places them properly in order of importance.

When we focus on Jesus (and this is what Paul is saying when he speaks of matters of first importance), we will discover that unity begins with our common relationship in Christ rather than resulting from conformity in things which are not of first importance.

Christian Attitudes

We have seen how negative attitudes contribute to sectarianism. Among these are the party spirit, dogmatism, and judgmentalism. Improper attitudes, as much as anything else, are at the heart of the problem. Here again, focusing on Jesus helps us put things in perspective.

Paul wrote the Philippians, "Have this mind among yourselves, which you have in Christ Jesus" (Phil. 2:5). The New International Version renders the verse, "Your attitude should be the same as that of Jesus Christ." This means that we must develop the same mind-set as Jesus.

As we study the gospels we learn how Jesus thought. He taught his disciples to treat others as they would like to be treated. Then he demonstrated this principle in his relationships with others. He instructed his followers to return good for evil and to overcome evil with good. He also showed us how to do this as he forgave his accusers when he was on the cross. He continually stressed the importance of loving others and gave us a perfect example by dying for us in the supreme expression of that love.

We cannot truly be Jesus' disciples unless we aspire to the characteristics reflected in those behaviors. This is difficult. It takes great effort to develop the mind of Christ. But we cannot afford to stop working toward that goal. Sectarian attitudes are a major hindrance in learning to think like Jesus. Consider how this is so.

The *party spirit* emerges when members of the party feel that they are the only ones who are right, or at least that they are more fully pleasing to God than are other Christians. This spirit tends to be self-centered, focusing more on the party than on the body of Christ as a whole. Even congregations divide because elements in the church have polarized around strong personalities. The factions are more interested in having their own way than in promoting the welfare of the local church. However, Jesus tells us to be selfless. If we have his mind and follow his teaching, we will be more concerned about the welfare of the entire body than in furthering our own sectarian interests.

Dogmatism grows out of a person's presumptuous perception that his views are totally correct and cannot be wrong. The religious dogmatist is often unwilling to admit that other interpretations of Scripture are even worthy of consideration. Since he believes that he has all the truth, or at least more than others, he decides that if others love God they must accept his understanding. If they do not, he concludes that they are unwilling to accept the truth because they do not love the Lord. There is an arrogance in the dogmatist which can be removed only by focusing on Jesus. The person with the mind of Christ is humble. He directs those whom he teaches to Jesus rather than to his own close reasoning and conclusions. This does not lessen his commitment to truth. To be committed to Jesus is to be committed to God's word. However, he is aware that no one has a monopoly on truth.

The very act of pointing others to Christ will help us overcome the sectarian spirit. It will also make those we teach more receptive to our message.

Judgmentalism usually accompanies the party spirit and dogmatism. The judgmental individual is quick to condemn, often without knowing all the facts. We all are judgmental at times. Judgmentalism can be spiritually devastating to the truth seeker who sees the teachings of Jesus contradicted by the judgmental attitudes of his would-be teacher. He may even declare, "If that's the spirit you have in your religion, I don't want any of it."

Again, Jesus is the corrective. When one focuses on Jesus, he hears Paul admonish him, "Who are you to pass judgment on the servant of another? It is before his own master that he stands or falls. . . . each of us shall give account of himself to God" (Rom. 14:4,12). The judgmental person looks to himself to judge others; the one with the mind of Christ is content to let Jesus do the judging.

The Sectarian Heart

Ultimately, sectarianism is a condition of the individual heart. A congregation beset by this malady only reflects the attitudes of its members. Christians with sectarian attitudes do not necessarily lack in spirituality. They may be caring people who deeply love the Lord and are determined to take his message to the lost. Nevertheless, their sectarianism will inevitably impede their efforts because they do not focus on Jesus.

If the problem of sectarianism is rooted in the heart, the solution is found by correcting the thinking to make Jesus preeminent in our faith. When each one is aware of his own misunderstandings, he will then "*look to Jesus the pioneer and perfecter of our faith*" to help him remove his sectarianism.

Footnotes

1. Monroe E. Hawley, *The Focus of Our Faith* (Nashville, TN: 20th Century Christian, 1985), p. 83.

2. Ira North, *Balance* (Nashville, TN: Gospel Advocate, 1983).